Mass Incarceration

KEYNOTES IN CRIMINOLOGY AND CRIMINAL JUSTICE SERIES

Keramet Reiter

New York   Oxford
OXFORD UNIVERSITY PRESS

Oxford University Press is a department of the University of Oxford. It furthers the University's objective of excellence in research, scholarship, and education by publishing worldwide. Oxford is a registered trade mark of Oxford University Press in the UK and certain other countries.

Published in the United States of America by Oxford University Press
198 Madison Avenue, New York, NY 10016, United States of America.

© 2018 by Oxford University Press

Library of Congress Cataloging-in-Publication Data

Names: Reiter, Keramet, author.
Title: Mass incarceration / Keramet Reiter.
Description: New York : Oxford University Press, 2017. | Series: Keynotes in criminology & criminal justice
Identifiers: LCCN 2017013363 (print) | LCCN 2017014245 (ebook) | ISBN 9780190647292 (ebook) | ISBN 9780190272531 (pbk.)
Subjects: LCSH: Criminal justice, Administration of—Political aspects—United States. | Prisoners—Legal status, laws, etc.—United States. | Imprisonment—United States. | Imprisonment—Political aspects—United States.
Classification: LCC KF9223 (ebook) | LCC KF9223 .R45 2017 (print) | DDC 365/.973—dc23
LC record available at https://lccn.loc.gov/2017013363

TABLE OF CONTENTS

Keynotes in Criminology and Criminal Justice Series

This Series is designed to provide essential knowledge on important contemporary matters of crime, law, and justice to a broad audience of readers including students, educators, researchers, and practitioners alike, and in a format that is not only authoritative, but highly engaging and concise. Nationally and internationally respected scholars share their knowledge and unique insights in comprehensive surveys and penetrating analyses of a variety of major contemporary issues central to the study of criminology, criminal justice, and social justice more generally. Forthcoming and planned Series books cover such areas as electronic crime, race, crime and justice, white-collar and corporate crime, violence in international perspective, gender and crime, gangs, mass incarceration, police and surveillance, financial fraud, and critical criminology.

I invite you to examine the Series and see how these readable, affordable, topical, and highly informative books can be used to help educate a new generation of students in understanding the social realities surrounding crime and justice in both domestic and global perspective.

Henry Pontell, Editor
Keynotes in Criminology and Criminal Justice Series
Distinguished Professor, John Jay College of Criminal Justice, CUNY
Professor Emeritus, University of California, Irvine

ACKNOWLEDGMENTS

This project was suggested and encouraged by Henry Pontell and shepherded through the publishing process by Steve Helba, who recruited a superlatively thorough and generous group of manuscript reviewers, including: Michelle Brown, University of Tennessee; Gina M. Caruolo, Williams University; Brenda Chaney, Ohio State University; Jennifer Cobbina, Michigan State University; Hayden Griffin, University of Alabama–Birmingham; Bruce Hoffman, Ohio University; Sandra Joy, Rowan University; EmmaLeigh Kirchner, Mercyhurst University; Jodi Lane, University of Florida; Breanne Pleggenkuhle, Southern Illinois University–Carbondale; Edward Rhine, Ohio State University; Arnold R. Waggoner, Rose State College; John Whitehead, East Tennessee State University. Their thoughtful critiques and suggestions for additions made this manuscript better, and working with Oxford University Press has been a true pleasure. Tom Blair and Katy Wolff kindly read this manuscript from beginning to end, providing critical and copyediting advice.

ABOUT THE AUTHOR

Keramet Reiter is an assistant professor in the Department of Criminology, Law and Society and at the School of Law at the University of California–Irvine. She is the author of *23/7: Pelican Bay Prison and the Rise of Long-Term Solitary Confinement* (Yale University Press, 2016) and the co-editor with Alexa Koenig of *Extreme Punishment: Comparative Studies in Detention, Incarceration, and Solitary Confinement* (Palgrave MacMillan Press, 2015). Her publications also include articles in the *California Law Review, Criminal Justice & Behavior, Law & Society Review, Qualitative Inquiry, South Atlantic Quarterly,* and op-eds in the *Los Angeles Times, Time Magazine,* and the *Washington Post.* She lives in Long Beach, California. Dr. Reiter was awarded the 2017 American Society of Criminology's Ruth Cavan Young Scholar Award, given to recognize outstanding scholarly contributions to the discipline of criminology by someone who has received their degree within the past five years.

INTRODUCTION

More than 2 million people are in prison and jail in the United States today; that is roughly equal to the population of the city of Houston, Texas, or the nation of Qatar. The U.S. incarceration rate is the highest in the world—50 percent greater than the incarceration rates in Rwanda and Russia, and 500 percent greater than China's incarceration rate.[1] Between 1972 and 2007, U.S. incarceration rates quintupled.[2] Between 1980 and 2015, the number of people in prisons and jails for drug offenses increased twelve-fold. In 2015, one in every ten black men in their thirties was incarcerated on any given day in the United States; for black men born in 2001, an estimated one in three will be incarcerated within their lifetimes.[3] Economists estimate that U.S. incarceration costs $75 billion dollars per year.[4] The phrase *mass incarceration* describes this large-scale phenomenon.

Mass incarceration took criminologists by surprise. In 1973, just as the phenomenon began, two eminent criminologists noted that

[1] Sentencing Project, "Fact Sheet: Trends in U.S. Corrections," http://sentencingproject. org/doc/publications/inc_Trends_in_Corrections_Fact_sheet.pdf.

[2] Franklin Zimring, "The Scale of Imprisonment in the United States: Twentieth Century Patterns and Twenty-First Century Prospects," *British Journal of Criminology* 100, no. 3 (2010): 1225–45, at 1228.

[3] Sentencing Project, "Fact Sheet: Trends."

[4] Vlogbrothers, "Mass Incarceration in the U.S." Apr. 4, 2014, https://www.youtube.com/watch?v=NaPBcUUqbew.

imprisonment rates appeared to be consistent over time, across the United States and in Europe.[5] That very year, however, imprisonment rates in the United States began their climb upwards. Ever since 1973, scholars have been trying to make sense of mass incarceration and its impact on specific individuals, institutions, and communities. Did Americans become less forgiving and more retributive? Did racism increase? Did crime rates increase?

Many people assume that incarceration is closely related to crime rates: rising crime rates might encourage rising incarceration, but rising incarceration, in turn, should reduce crime. However, criminologists have found that the two are barely related.[6] Instead, scholars from a variety of disciplines have suggested other, more nuanced (macro-level) explanations for mass incarceration. Legal scholars argue that sentencing policy changes and excessive attention to process and procedures (instead of to substantive justice) drove incarceration rates up.[7] Criminologists argue that declining faith in the ideal of rehabilitation, fear of crime, and politicians who act tough on crime in order to attract voters all contributed to rising incarceration rates.[8] Sociologists and geographers argue that mass incarceration resulted from oppression of racial minorities, high unemployment rates, and the criminalization of poverty, especially through

[5] Alfred Blumstein and Jacqueline Cohen, "A Theory of the Stability of Punishment," *Journal of Criminal Law and Criminology* 64, no. 2 (1973): 198–207.

[6] Franklin E. Zimring, *The Great American Crime Decline* (New York: Oxford University Press, 2007); see also Steven D. Levitt, "Understanding Why Crime Fell in the 1990s: Four Factors that Explain the Decline and Six that Do Not," *Journal of Economic Perspectives* 18, no. 1 (Winter 2004): 163–90.

[7] See, e.g., Michael Tonry, *Sentencing Reform Impacts* (Washington, D.C.: National Institute of Justice, 1987); Alfred Blumstein, "Prison Populations: A System Out of Control," in *Crime and Justice: A Review of Research*, vol. 10, Michael Tonry and Norval Morris, eds. (Chicago: University of Chicago Press, 1988); David Garland, *Culture of Control: Crime and Social Order in Contemporary Society* (Chicago: University of Chicago Press, 2001); William J. Stuntz, "The Political Constitution of Criminal Justice," *Harvard Law Review* 119, no. 3 (Jan. 2006): 780–851, at 783; Frank Zimring and Gordon Hawkins, *The Scale of Imprisonment* (Chicago: University of Chicago Press, 1991).

[8] Blumstein, "Prison Populations"; Garland, *Culture of Control*; Jonathan Simon, *Governing Through Crime: How the War on Crime Transformed American Democracy and Created a Culture of Fear* (New York: Oxford University Press, 2007).

the War on Drugs.[9] Anthropologists and historians argue that mass incarceration has been wielded as a tool of control against certain categories of people: to manage the mentally ill, for instance, and to constrain organized African-American resistance to oppression.[10] And political scientists argue that the short-term thinking and goals of neoliberal politicians, as well as restrictions on the citizenship rights of certain groups of people, have reinforced mass incarceration.[11]

A phenomenon as complex as a nation's decision to incarcerate millions of people over decades turns out to be difficult to reduce to a singular explanation, like economic pressures or racist policies. For this reason, this book integrates multiple disciplinary approaches—drawing on theories and evidence from economics to sociology to political science to philosophy—to make sense of mass incarceration. The common thread throughout this interdisciplinary approach is legal: readers of this book will gain familiarity with major legal cases and basic legal principles structuring mass incarceration, and will explore fundamental questions about the relationship between law, (in)equality, and (in)justice. Focusing on legal cases, litigation, and rights permits an examination of macro-level trends in incarceration over time in relation to micro-level experiences of imprisonment.

[9] Ruth Wilson Gilmore, *Golden Gulag: Prisons, Surplus, Crisis, and Opposition in Globalizing California* (Berkeley: University of California Press, 2007); Loïc Wacquant, *The Place of the Prison in the New Government* (Minneapolis: University of Minnesota Press, 2006); Loïc Wacquant, "Deadly Symbiosis: When Ghetto and Prison Meet and Mesh," *Punishment & Society* 3, no. 1 (2001): 95–134; Loïc Wacquant, *Urban Outcasts: A Comparative Sociology of Advanced Marginality* (Malden: Polity Press 2008).

[10] On mental illness, see Lorna Rhodes, *Total Confinement: Madness and Reason in the Maximum Security Prison* (Berkeley: University of California Press, 2004); Jonathan Metzl, *The Protest Psychosis: How Schizophrenia Became a Black Disease* (Boston: Beacon Press, 2011). On black organizing and resistance, see Damien Sojoyner, *First Strike: Educational Enclosures in Black Los Angeles* (Minneapolis: University of Minnesota Press, 2016); Dan Berger, *Captive Nation: Black Prison Organizing in the Civil Rights Era* (Chapel Hill: University of North Carolina Press, 2014); Heather Ann Thompson, *Blood in the Water: The Attica Prison Uprising of 1971* (New York: Pantheon, 2016).

[11] Marie Gottschalk, *The Prison and the Gallows: The Politics of Mass Incarceration in America* (Cambridge, UK: Cambridge University Press, 2006); Marie Gottschalk, *Caught: The Prison State and the Lockdown of American Politics* (Princeton: Princeton University Press, 2015).

Understanding mass incarceration, especially at the "micro" level, requires not only an interdisciplinary perspective, but a basic knowledge of the goals of punishment, and whether or not they are being achieved. Specifically, why do legislators write laws defining crimes and establishing punishments associated with those crimes? And how do juries and judges calibrate and impose prison sentences on lawbreakers? Traditionally, both legislators and jurists justify punishment on either "moral" or "utilitarian" grounds.

Moral, or *retributive*, justifications for punishment focus on right and wrong, describing punishment as the appropriate response to lawbreaking, or as the fair thing to do. One classic retributive justification for punishment is the idea of "an eye for an eye": if you poke someone's eye out, that person has a right to poke your eye out in retaliation, or at least to be compensated in proportion to the severity of the harm suffered. Utilitarian justifications, by contrast, include *deterrence, rehabilitation*, and *incapacitation*.[12] These justifications focus on using punishment to achieve certain outcomes, such as: discouraging future misbehavior or lawbreaking with the threat of consequences (deterrence); reforming individuals through training, education, or treatment, so that they no longer misbehave or commit crimes (rehabilitation); and warehousing criminals to ensure that they are not able to violate or hurt people in their communities (incapacitation).

One additional, more modern justification for punishment interweaves moral and utilitarian goals in an effort to achieve not just rehabilitation of an offender, but reparation of harm, for victims as well as offenders. *Restorative justice* seeks to provide both victims and offenders a voice in designing punishments that are meant to re-establish shared values and heal the emotional, financial, and social wounds crime can create. The most common form of restorative justice is "victim-offender mediation,"

---

[12] For thoughtful overviews of these theories of punishment and the moral versus utilitarian debates, see John Rawls, "Two Concepts of Rules (1955)," in *The Philosophy of Punishment: A Collection of Papers*, H. B. Acton, ed. (New York: Macmillan, St. Martin's Press, 1969): 105–114; H.L.A. Hart, "The Presidential Address: Prolegomenon to the Principles of Punishment," *Proceedings of the Aristotelian Society, New Series* 60 (1959–60): 1–26.

where community stakeholders, perpetrators, and those harmed by crime come together to discuss what happened, who was hurt, and to agree on some restorative action—like cleaning up graffiti, apologizing publicly, or participating in a treatment program. John Braithwaite, one of the main theorists of restorative justice, summed up the philosophy: "because crime hurts, justice should heal."[13]

Lawmakers, judges, and prison officials all reference these justifications for punishment. For instance, in passing a law that calls for the death penalty for premeditated murder, legislators might argue that the law is the only just response to a violent act (retribution) and that ensuring that people who plan murder face severe punishments will discourage future offenders from behaving that way (deterrence). These competing justifications for punishment provide a framework for evaluating not only why and how punishments are imposed, but also whether punishments are either fair or effective. In the chapters that follow, consider what purposes various aspects of punishment are trying to achieve, and whether these purposes are, indeed, being achieved.

ON (IN)VISIBILITY

Mass incarceration has captured the attention of the popular media, spurring an industry catering to the cultural fascination with incarceration. Journalists, filmmakers, and authors have eagerly explored the increasingly common experience of imprisonment—from the possibilities of escape (chronicled in the television series *Prison Break* and the 2013 action movie *Escape Plan* starring Sylvester Stallone and Arnold Schwarzenegger, for instance) to the trials and tribulations of everyday life (as revealed in the National Geographic documentary series *Lockdown* and the bestselling book and popular Netflix series *Orange is the New Black*). At first glance, then, mass incarceration is a highly visible

---

[13] John Braithwaite, "Restorative Justice and De-Professionalization," *The Good Society* 13, no. 1 (2004): 28–31. See also John Braithwaite, *Crime, Shame and Reintegration* (Cambridge, UK: Cambridge University Press, 1989).

phenomenon—affecting millions of people, costing billions of dollars, and consistently attracting all sorts of media attention.

However, these *visible* aspects of mass incarceration represent only the tip of the iceberg. Many aspects of mass incarceration have remained *invisible* over the last forty years. This invisibility results from three key aspects of U.S. prisons: their geographic isolation, their structural diffusion, and their administrative status. First, many of the prisons built over the last forty years have been built in out-of-the-way, rural locations.[14] This means that lawyers and judges, legislators and journalists, doctors and researchers—not to mention prisoners' families—face significant challenges in visiting, observing, and investigating America's prisons. Second, the U.S. prison system actually encompasses fifty-one different prison systems: one federal system and fifty separate state systems. Increasingly, sentences for violating the law also include a range of sanctions beyond incarceration in one of these fifty-one prison systems, including: incarceration in local jail facilities (of which there are 3,283 across the United States[15]), fines and fees levied on top of (or instead of) incarceration, and the use of electronic monitoring or other forms of surveillance outside of secure facilities.[16]

---

[14] Ruth Wilson Gilmore, *Golden Gulag: Prisons, Surplus, Crisis, and Opposition in Globalizing California* (Berkeley: University of California Press, 2007); Gilmore, *Golden Gulag*; Eric Lotke and Peter Wagner, "The Modern American Penal System: Prisoners of the Census: Electoral and Financial Consequences of Counting Prisoners Where They Go, Not Where They Come From," *Pace Law Review* 24 (2005): 587–607.

[15] Peter Wagner and Bernadette Rabuy, "Mass Incarceration: The Whole Pie, 2016," *Prison Policy Initiative*, Mar. 14, 2016, https://www.prisonpolicy.org/reports/pie2016.html.

[16] For a discussion of the expanding scope of these punitive sanctions and the importance of conceptualizing mass incarceration broadly to include a range of sanctions, see Michelle Phelps, "Mass Probation: Toward a More Robust Theory of State Variation in Punishment," *Punishment & Society* 19, no. 1 (2017): 53–73. Traditionally, prisons hold people sentenced to a period of incarceration of one year or more, while jails hold people who are either awaiting sentencing, or who have been sentenced to less than one year. See Bureau of Justice Statistics, "FAQ Detail: What is the difference between jails and prisons?" https://www.bjs.gov/index.cfm?ty=qa&iid=322. However, this distinction has been blurred in many states in recent years. For instance, in California, people convicted of nonviolent crimes can spend years incarcerated in local jail facilities instead of being transferred to overcrowded state prison facilities. For a description of this phenomenon across multiple states, see Brian Albert, *State Prisoners in County Jails* (Washington, D.C.: National Association of Counties, 2010), http://www.naco.org/sites/default/files/documents/State%20Prisoners%20in%20County%20Jails%20Updated.pdf.

As a result, collecting consistent data and comparing such data across different jurisdictions and categories of sanctions is challenging. Third, individual U.S. prisons are administratively complex institutions; the warden or superintendent in charge of any given prison (or local jail) usually has discretion in how he or she treats and manages both prisoners and staff. Few requirements exist for the collection and distribution of basic information about prison operations and procedures.[17] Together, these geographic, structural, and administrative factors have shaped the phenomenon of mass incarceration.

The invisibility of many of the more disturbing aspects of mass incarceration creates numerous challenges both in describing the basic attributes of who is incarcerated and in analyzing the impacts of this incarceration on individuals, institutions, and communities. By examining both individual, micro-level experiences and social science, macro-level analyses in five key aspects of mass incarceration, this book seeks to provide a framework for rendering mass incarceration both more visible and more susceptible to rigorous evaluation, in terms of both effectiveness and fairness.

BOOK STRUCTURE AND SOURCES

In five succinct chapters, this book explores some of the least visible, but arguably most important, characteristics of mass incarceration in the United States: (1) the systematic constriction of prisoners' constitutional rights, (2) the treatment of the mentally ill in prison and especially in solitary confinement, (3) the long-term consequences of having served time in prison, (4) the problem of prisoner disenfranchisement, and (5) the privatization of multiple aspects of the prison industry. Each chapter begins with a narrative account of one individual's experience within the prison system, drawn from actual cases and recent events, which frames the history, themes, and core ethical questions addressed in that chapter. Different disciplinary perspectives on mass incarceration thread through each chapter and generate distinct policy questions.

---

[17] Keramet Reiter, "Making Windows in Walls: Strategies for Prison Research," *Qualitative Inquiry* 20, no. 4 (Apr. 2014): 417–28.

This book is designed to be clear and accessible as an introduction to punishment and mass incarceration for students in a variety of disciplinary fields. However, by providing links to many additional resources, the book is also intended as a launch pad for more nuanced theoretical debates and complex policy analyses. The examples, sources, and footnotes have been carefully selected to provide a range of possibilities for further reading and exploration: from news stories and concise policy reports to government investigations, accessible academic articles, YouTube videos and documentaries, and interactive Internet sites. Such additional sources might supplement the text in both classroom and research environments.

CHAPTER PREVIEWS

Chapter One examines prisoners' constitutional rights. This chapter begins with a description of the facts of the U.S. Supreme Court case *Hope v. Pelzer* (2002). Larry Hope, an Alabama prisoner, alleged he had been abused by prison guards, by being chained outside for hours at a time to a "hitching post"—an immobilizing bar better known for its use on African-American slaves in the nineteenth century than for its use on prisoners in the twenty-first century. The chapter first examines the explicit and implicit purposes of the hitching post, and then situates Larry Hope's legal challenge in the broader context of the history of the disparate treatment of African-Americans in U.S. prisons and of the socio-legal trends in litigation over prison conditions. Prisoner lawsuits force prison systems to balance basic rights, like demands for humane and equal treatment, against problems of institutional management, like the need to maintain safety and security. The chapter asks:

- What rights should prisoners have?
- What tools should prisoners have with which to assert their rights?

Chapter Two focuses on the challenges of providing basic healthcare (especially mental healthcare) within a prison. The chapter begins with the story of Joseph Duran, a seriously mentally and physically ill prisoner, who died of asphyxiation, alone in a California prison cell, in September of 2013. In spite of ongoing litigation evaluating the treatment of mentally ill prisoners in California prisons, Duran's death was only reported after a whistleblower from within the prison system provided records of the case to a major California newspaper. Understanding how and why Duran ended up not only in prison, but in solitary confinement, provides a framework for examining both the psychological consequences of incarceration and the interactions between social welfare policies (like when and how healthcare is provided) with punitive policies (like who goes to prison and how they are treated there). Whereas Chapter One raises questions about what rights prisoners should have, this chapter asks:

- What obligations should prison officials have to prisoners?
- What should the relationship be between prisons and other social institutions, like hospitals and the media?

Chapter Three documents the longer-term impacts of mass incarceration, including: a web of punishments beyond imprisonment, the lasting stigma of having been imprisoned, and the damages suffered by the family members and communities of currently and formerly imprisoned people. The chapter begins with the story of Howard Bailey, a Jamaican immigrant and U.S. Navy veteran, who served fifteen months in prison on a marijuana trafficking charge, after which he painstakingly re-built his family life and personal business, before applying for U.S. citizenship. His citizenship application triggered his deportation to Jamaica as a consequence of his earlier felony drug conviction. Bailey's story reveals how a range of *collateral consequences* interact to amplify punishment. Most collateral consequences, however, are not legally categorized as punishments. This means that people like Bailey cannot challenge a consequence like deportation under the Eighth Amendment prohibition against cruel and unusual *punishment*. This chapter draws on a range of historical and sociological analyses to outline both the scope and scale of collateral consequences. Instead of focusing on the rights of prisoners, or the obligations of prison officials, however, this chapter asks:

- What counts as punishment, and how much punishment is too much?
- How can the costs of punishment be measured, and how can these costs be weighed against the benefits of punishment?

Chapter Four focuses on one particular collateral consequence of mass incarceration—felony disenfranchisement—and examines its political implications. The chapter begins with the story of Eileen Janis, a Native American, who was mistakenly turned away from voting in the 2008 presidential election because of a prior felony conviction for which she had served five years on probation. As with Larry Hope, Joseph Duran, and Howard Bailey, Janis's experience represents the culmination of decades of oppressive and exclusionary policies: in this case, policies excluding any felon from participating in democratic society. This chapter explores the political impacts, on everything from census counts to election outcomes, of *disenfranchising* certain groups of people. Felony disenfranchisement policies have created pockets of political silence among disproportionately affected minority groups. These policies have also created pockets of exaggerated influence among disproportionately benefitted census tracts, where prisoners count towards electoral vote allocations, even though these prisoners cannot vote. This chapter steps back to ask not just how mass incarceration affects individuals and families, but also society:

- How does mass incarceration affect democratic structures and policies?
- Is re-enfranchisement possible, and what would be the implications?

Chapter Five examines mass incarceration from an economic perspective, looking at who profits from prison policies and querying whether profits distort justice. Instead of focusing on someone experiencing an injustice as a result of mass incarceration policies, this chapter begins with the story of T. Don Hutto, an architect of mass incarceration policies. After a decades-long career in corrections, running prison systems in Arkansas and Virginia, in 1983, Hutto became a cofounder of the leading private prison company in the United States: Corrections Corporation of America. As director of CCA, he negotiated dozens of government contracts to privatize incarceration in local jail and state prison facilities. This chapter identifies the many "players" in the prison industry, such as Hutto; "payers," such as family members of prisoners; and "profiteers," such as private corporations and politicians negotiating contracts to operate private prisons. The chapter asks:

- How are economic motives reconciled with legal obligations?
- Can a profitable prison system also serve justice, and, if so, under what conditions?

In the conclusion, the themes of legal rights, (in)equality, and (in)justice are revisited in light of the stories and cases at the heart of each of these five chapters. In order to provide a historical overview of the phenomenon of mass incarceration, a timeline of key events and legal cases, as well as references to the people and stories profiled in the five main chapters, appears at the end of the conclusion.

This book reaches past the nonviolent drug offender, the innocent, and the deserving, to focus on the more difficult cases of the prisoners who did commit crimes, were difficult to deal with, and perhaps might be considered to deserve their punishments. Focusing on these "trouble cases," the following chapters ask what individuals' experiences are in prison, what rights they have, and what rights they should have.[18] The following pages contain many vivid and detailed stories of injustice, physical and mental

---

[18] The idea of the "trouble case" comes from the classic legal anthropological work *The Cheyenne Way: Conflict and Case Law in Primitive Jurisprudence*, about Native American legal systems, by Karl N. Llewellyn and E. Adamson Hoebel (New York: William S. Hein & Company, 1941). For an analysis of the importance of "trouble cases" in law and society scholarship, see Austin Sarat, ed., *Everyday Practices and Trouble Cases: Fundamental Issues in Law and Society Research*, Vol. 2 (Chicago: Northwestern University Press, 1998).

abuse, and practices that arguably constitute torture. The stories are not meant to be sensational, however.

Nonetheless, writing about brutality presents an ethical conundrum— the first of many this book seeks to highlight. Am I simply writing to attract your attention, to compel you not only to stare, but to become a voyeur into other people's private sufferings, as you would rubbernecking at a tragic car accident on the other side of the highway? I hope not.

These stories are intended, first, to command your attention and to linger in your memory. They are intended, second, to represent the seriousness and frequency of abuse in U.S. prisons. Finally, they are meant to transform abstract moral questions and vague legal rights into real-world examples that concretely frame the practical implications of this or that decision, policy, or law.

[1]

THE EXCEPTION TO EVERY RULE: CONSTITUTIONAL EXEMPTIONS AND LIMITATIONS

Over the last forty years, U.S. courts have systematically limited the rights that prisoners have under the U.S. Constitution. Some scholars have compared modern U.S. prisoners to nineteenth century U.S. slaves, prisoners' rights are so limited.[1] U.S. courts have held that prisoners can only exercise fundamental rights, like the rights to freedom of speech and association, *if* exercising those rights does not compromise the safety and security of the prison.[2] And courts reviewing prisoner claims about unconstitutional conditions of confinement rarely contradict prison administrators' assertions about what is required for safety and security.

In order to establish a constitutional violation, prisoners like Larry Hope, who claimed that Alabama officials violated his fundamental rights by chaining him to a hitching post for seven hours in 1995, must prove that prison administrators actually knew and also deliberately ignored any risks of abuse or harm.[3] This dual requirement of both knowledge and willful disregard of that knowledge is known as the *deliberate indifference* standard.[4] This chapter begins with the story of Larry Hope's years-long

---

[1] See, e.g., Colin Dayan, *The Story of Cruel and Unusual* (Cambridge, MA: MIT Press, 2007).

[2] John Boston and Daniel Manville, *Prisoners' Self-Help Litigation Manual*, 4th ed. (New York: Oxford University Press, 2010).

[3] Sharon Dolovich, "Forms of Deference in Prison Law," *Federal Sentencing Reporter* 24, no. 4 (Apr. 2012): 245–59.

[4] In order to win a remedy or compensation for inadequate care or abuse, a nonprisoner usually must prove negligence, which does not necessarily require proof of either knowledge of a specific risk or willful disregard of that risk. Prisoners, however, must prove a more obvious and egregious harm in order to establish deliberate indifference. By requiring more proof to establish harm to prisoners than nonprisoners, the deliberate indifference standard essentially creates a lower "standard of care" in prisons.

journey to hold Alabama prison officials accountable for the abuse he experienced, then works backward to provide an overview of how prisoners' rights have been expanded and constrained over the twentieth century. The chapter ends with an examination of two recent cases in California, which have mandated improvements in prison conditions in the state. Throughout, this chapter examines what rights prisoners have, asks what rights prisoners should have, and evaluates the costs and benefits of expanding (or contracting) rights.

LARRY HOPE

Larry Hope fell asleep on the bus ride to his prison worksite at the Limestone Correctional Facility in Harvest, Alabama, in June of 1995. He was slow to wake up when the bus stopped at the worksite, frustrating the guards; "a wrestling match" ensued between Hope and a guard. Guards "placed" Hope in handcuffs and leg irons and transported him back to the Limestone prison. Then, as punishment for his disruptiveness, prison guards tied Hope to a hitching post, shirtless, outside in the summer sun. Guards left Hope out, chained, without food, water, or access to a bathroom, for seven hours.[5]

According to prison officials, Hope was not exactly a model prisoner, or citizen. He had been chained to the hitching post once before, in May of 1995, after he got into an argument with another prisoner with whom he was working on a *chain gang*—a form of punishment deployed in the southern United States in the late nineteenth and early twentieth centuries, abandoned in the 1950s, and reintroduced in the 1990s.[6] That first

---

[5] *Hope v. Pelzer*, 536 U.S. 730, 735 (2002).

[6] Chain gangs in the 2010s remained relatively rare and were in use in only a few jurisdictions, like Maricopa County in Arizona, notorious for its tough-on-crime Sheriff Joe Arpaio, who served from 1993 to 2016, and attracted attention for live-streaming videos of detainees' holding cells, forcing jail detainees to wear pink underwear and flip flops and to live in tent cities, and arresting journalists who dared to write critically about his policies. Michael Kiefer, "Sheriff Joe Arpaio Has Always Done It His Way," *Arizona Republic*, Sept. 11, 2015, http://www.azcentral.com/story/news/arizona/investigations/2015/09/11/sheriff-joe-arpaio-legacy/71888720/; Mindy Sink, "Life from Arizona: Inmates on the Web," *Baltimore Sun*, Aug. 28, 2000, http://articles.baltimoresun.com/2000-08-28/entertainment/0008260001_1_cams-arpaio-maricopa-county. For images of the Maricopa County chain gangs, see Jessica Jerreat, "'It Looks Like 21st Century Slavery':

time, though, Hope was only chained to the hitching post for two hours, and prison documents suggest he was offered water and bathroom breaks a few times an hour.[7] (Hope was serving a life sentence for rape.[8])

The "hitching post" used on Hope in Alabama in 1995 was a metal bar, about chest high—four to five feet from the ground, with rings hanging from it. Hope's arms would have been cuffed one to a ring, and he would have been immobilized, hands raised above his shoulders, for hours at a time. The Supreme Court would later note the "obvious" brutality of the practice. It was physically risky, too: hours on the hitching post in Southern summer sun risked causing both internal muscle injury and medically significant sunburning.[9] The image of an African-American man cuffed, shirtless, to a hitching post is something the average American might expect to see in a history textbook, describing slavery on a Southern plantation. Instead, cuffing prisoners to hitching posts was apparently standard practice in Alabama into the late 1990s.

Larry Hope's case actually stemmed from a bigger class action lawsuit brought by a group of Alabama prisoners, who argued that many aspects of their treatment in prison violated the Eighth Amendment prohibition against cruel and unusual punishment. In the class action case of *Austin v. Hopper* (later *Austin v. James*), prisoners challenged: the use of chain gangs, the use of hitching posts, and the denial of adequate toilet facilities.[10] Specifically, prisoners working on chain gangs in Alabama were tethered together in groups of five; assigned to work ten-hour shifts along Alabama highways picking up trash, mowing grass, and breaking

Photographer's Images of Arizona's Chain Gangs Evoke a Dark Period in the Country's History," *The Guardian*, Jan. 29, 2014, http://www.dailymail.co.uk/news/article-2547778/Images-Arizona-chain-gang-evoke-dark-history-slavery.html. For descriptions of the use of chain gangs in southern prisons over time, see Mitchel P. Roth, *Prisons and Prison Systems: A Global Encyclopedia* (Westport, CT: Greenwood Press, 2006); Alex Lichtenstein, "Good Roads and Chain Gangs in the Progressive South: 'The Negro Convict is a Slave,'" *Journal of Southern History* 59, no. 1 (1993): 85–110.

[7] *Hope v. Pelzer*, 536 U.S. at 735.

[8] Associated Press, "Judge Rejects Suit by Alabama Inmate Handcuffed to Hitching Post," *Tuscaloosa News*, Nov. 9, 2005, 3B.

[9] *Hope v. Pelzer*, 536 U.S. at 742.

[10] "Chain Gang and Hitching Post Case," Southern Poverty Law Center, https://www.splcenter.org/seeking-justice/case-docket/austin-v-james.

up rocks; and were expected to use the bathroom while chained, with no privacy, no toilet paper, and no way to wash their hands. Prisoners who refused to work (or who otherwise offended prison guards) were chained to the hitching post. Larry Hope, it turned out, was far from alone in his experience of an extended shift bound to the post with no food, water, or bathroom access.

In reviewing the claims of Larry Hope and his fellow prisoners, Alabama federal district court judge Myron Thompson, renowned for his liberal politics in an otherwise conservative state, could barely contain his outrage. In the first page of his opinion reviewing the prisoners' claims, Judge Thompson noted the "sordid" history of chain gangs in the South:

> During the Reconstruction era, chain gangs provided an alternative to rebuilding the penal institutions that were destroyed during the Civil War; they also served as a cheap form of labor. The majority of these chain-gang inmates, who died at enormously high rates due to the brutal conditions, were African-Americans . . . Chain gangs were later incorporated into the convict-lease system, whose atrocities have been well-documented[:] "For the Southern convict-lease system a modern scholar can 'find parallel only in the persecutions of the Middle Ages or in the prison camps of Nazi Germany.'"[11]

Unsurprisingly, Judge Thompson upheld a settlement eliminating the use of chain gangs, and he ultimately oversaw the elimination of the hitching post, too. Once all of these conditions of confinement disputes were finally settled in 1998, Larry Hope filed his own lawsuit seeking damages from specific prison guards for the way they treated him those times he was tethered to that hitching post, which Judge Thompson had found to be unconstitutional, and which Alabama had agreed to stop using.

Unfortunately for Hope, his individual claim for damages did not land in Judge Thompson's (sympathetic) court. (Hope had been moved to a different prison, in a different judicial district.) Instead, a magistrate judge in

[11] *Austin v. Hopper*, 15 F. Supp. 2d 1210, 1215 (M.D. Ala. 1998).

central Alabama reviewed Hope's claims. Judge Ott determined that, at the time Hope was tethered to that hitching post in May and June of 1995, the law about whether or not the practice violated the Eighth Amendment was ambiguous.[12] After all, the class action case about the issue was not settled until 1998. This meant the prison guards were entitled to claim *qualified immunity* from being sued.

In a case where there is some ambiguity as to a legal question, like whether or not a hitching post is constitutional, government officials, like prison guards, have a right to claim immunity from being individually sued and being subject to orders to pay damages. This immunity is meant to protect the ability of government officials to exercise reasonable discretion in doing their jobs, day to day. Prison guards and police officers, especially, cannot be expected to keep up with every single legal change governing the rights of prisoners and citizens. Trained lawyers can hardly do that. Without qualified immunity, jurists argue, no one would be willing to do government work, for fear of being personally sued by any citizen who disliked a legal outcome. Police officers, prosecutors, and judges, who frequently impose adverse legal outcomes, such as arresting people or sentencing people to prison, would be especially vulnerable to lawsuits, absent the protection of some form of immunity. So, in response to Hope's allegations that he was treated unconstitutionally, the Alabama prison guards said they were exercising reasonable discretion in doing their jobs, and the hitching post was in wide use and not unconstitutional. Judge Ott agreed.[13]

Larry Hope and his lawyers disagreed. While the question of whether the hitching post was cruel and unusual had not been explicitly addressed in 1995, when Hope was tethered to it, Judge Thompson had noted that Hope's experience was one of the "most egregious examples of... abuse" in the record of the *Austin* case. And, even before that, in 1994, the U.S. Department of Justice had chastised Alabama prison officials for using a hitching post in another Alabama prison, and ordered the prison to cease using the device entirely.[14] On this basis, Hope and his lawyers appealed

---

[12] *Hope v. Pelzer,* No. CV-96-BU-2968-S (M.D. Ala. Mar. 24, 2000).
[13] Ibid.
[14] *Austin v. Hopper,* 15 F. Supp. 2d at 1247, 1249.

Judge Ott's decision to the Eleventh Circuit court of appeals, which over-sees federal cases from Alabama, Georgia, and Florida. The Eleventh Circuit, however, agreed with Judge Ott. Then, in 2001, something surprising happened. The Supreme Court agreed to hear Hope's appeal.

Each year, the U.S. Supreme Court receives thousands of *petitions for writs of certiorari* (between five thousand and seven thousand annually, to be exact), asking for review of a lower court decision. Of these petitions, the Court agrees to reconsider lower court decisions, less than 5 percent of the time—that's a few hundred cases a year, at most.[15] And, in a given year, the Court usually only hears one or two cases brought by or on behalf of prisoners. So when the Court agreed to hear Hope's case in 2001, Hope might as well have won the lottery.

When the case was argued before the U.S. Supreme Court in April of 2002, even the conservative Bush administration joined Larry Hope's side. The Bush administration lawyers argued, with Hope's lawyers, that prison guards in Alabama should have known that they were treating Hope cruelly, in violation of the Eighth Amendment. And they argued that those prison guards should not be shielded from liability—in other words, they should not be entitled to qualified immunity.[16] The U.S. Supreme Court agreed and ordered the courts in Alabama to re-consider Hope's claim that his rights had been egregiously violated.[17]

Prisoners' rights advocates celebrated the victory. Richard Cohen, a lawyer with the Southern Poverty Law Center, which had brought the class action case in *Austin* challenging the chain gangs and the hitching posts originally, said triumphantly: "This will put an end to the state's sorry history of using a torture device." Likewise, the *Washington Post* proclaimed: "Supreme Court Outlaws Ala. Prison Punishment."[18]

[15] Adam Feldman and Alexander Kappner, "Finding Certainty in Cert: An Empirical Analysis of the Factors Involved in Supreme Court Certiorari Decisions from 2001–15," *Villanova Law Review* 61, no. 5 (2017): 795–842.

[16] Linda Greenhouse, "U.S. Joins Inmate in Prison Discipline Case," *New York Times*, Apr. 18, 2002, www.nytimes.com/2002/04/18/us/us-joins-inmate-in-prison-discipline-case.html.

[17] *Hope v. Pelzer*, 536 U.S. 730 (2002).

[18] Mark Niesse, "Supreme Court Outlaws Ala. Prison Punishment," *Washington Post*, Jun. 28, 2002, https://www.washingtonpost.com/archive/politics/2002/06/28/supreme-court-out laws-ala-prison-punishment/88b2d040-484b-444c-9dc1-5be9abef9542/.

But would this matter for Larry Hope's lawsuit? Overcoming a claim of qualified immunity is only the first step for a prisoner seeking to hold prison officials liable for harm he has suffered. The second step is proving that prison officials acted with *deliberate indifference*: they knew they were causing harm, and they did it anyway.[19] Hope, then, had to go back to those same unsympathetic courts in Alabama and try again to convince them to hold those prison guards liable for the pain he suffered tied to those hitching posts. In 2005, Hope's case went to trial, in front of a jury, in Birmingham, Alabama. But Judge Bowdre dismissed the case before the jury ever had a chance to consider its merits. According to Bowdre, Hope had failed to prove that the prison guards who tied him to the hitching post knew they were causing him harm. He had failed to prove that they had acted with deliberate indifference to his well-being.[20] So ended a decade of Larry Hope seeking to have a court recognize the pain he suffered in 1995, and to hold the specific prison guards who had inflicted that pain responsible for their actions.

Larry Hope's case represents the challenges prisoners face in asserting basic rights. First, Hope's case reveals how egregiously a prisoner must be treated before he even has a chance of getting courts to pay attention. Second, his case reveals that, even once egregious treatment is established, an individual prisoner may never be able to recover damages for that treatment. Finally, the aftermath of Hope's case reveals that even years of litigation and critical national attention can fail to bring justice, or reform prison conditions.

In fact, in the era of mass incarceration, the severe limitations on prisoners' ability to challenge the conditions of their confinement, and to hold prison officials responsible for constitutional violations, functionally hides many abuses happening deep inside prison walls. Even though concepts like "qualified immunity" and "deliberate indifference" were meant to protect prison officials from being overwhelmed by frivolous lawsuits, they function in practice as roadblocks, keeping prisoners from asserting and winning claims about unconstitutional conditions of confinement. (Consider the years Hope spent establishing that his rights had been violated and seeking

---

[19] Dolovich, "Forms of Deference."
[20] Associated Press, "Judge Rejects Suit."

redress for the violations, and then imagine what other rights violations might exist, un-established and un-redressed, behind U.S. prison walls.)

Recent research suggests that rights violations have continued in Alabama prisons, in spite of the class-action litigation in *Austin* and Larry Hope's individual litigation. In 2008, three years after Hope's case finally concluded, a book exposed newly horrible conditions of confinement at Limestone Correctional Facility, the prison where Hope had been tied to the hitching post in 1995. Limestone prison officials were no longer using those hitching posts to immobilize prisoners. Instead, prison officials had implemented a new policy: segregating all HIV-positive prisoners in the state in Dorm 16 at Limestone—and chaining them to their beds.[21] In the early 2000s, roughly one prisoner a month was dying in Dorm 16, and none were receiving any end-of-life care or emergency medical treatment.[22]

If federal courts had to tell Alabama prison officials not to tie prisoners to hitching posts in 1998, and order those officials to provide those same prisoners with medical treatment in the 2000s, are other basic rights also going unmet? Prisoner lawsuits encompass everything from what kinds of books prisoners can possess to whether they were charged too much for snacks ordered from the prison canteen. Although not all prisoner lawsuits concern racist abuse or lethally inadequate healthcare, careful reviews of prisoner-initiated litigation suggest that the vast majority of legal challenges filed by prisoners concern potentially serious circumstances like assaults, inadequate medical and mental care, and dangerously unhygienic conditions.[23] The serious nature of Larry Hope's allegations, then, is far from exceptional. Often, however, multiple prisoners have to die, journalists and lawyers have to take notice, and courts have to weigh in before reform is even proposed, let alone implemented.

Why are basic human rights seemingly suspended in so many prisons? More specifically, why was it so hard for Larry Hope to get justice?

[21] Benjamin Fleury-Steiner, with Carla Crowder, *Dying Inside: The HIV/AIDS Ward at Limestone Prison* (Ann Arbor: University of Michigan, 2008).

[22] Karen Middleton, "Lawsuit Slows AIDS Death March At LCF," *News Courier*, Sept. 9, 2006, https://www.schr.org/node/117.

[23] Margo Schlanger, "Inmate Litigation," *Harvard Law Review* 116, no. 6 (2003): 1555–1706, 1570–73.

FROM SLAVES OF THE STATE TO MASTERS OF THE LAW?

Larry Hope might have faced a few (ultimately insurmountable) challenges in trying to hold Alabama prison officials responsible for tying him to a hitching post. But he was exercising a relatively new set of rights—to file a complaint about his conditions of confinement and to have a judge consider that complaint—to which prisoners had not been entitled for the first two centuries of America's existence. Originally, the U.S. Constitution codified only one basic right for convicted criminals: habeas corpus. The right to file a writ of *habeas corpus*, a Latin term which literally means "you shall have the body," dates back to medieval England. In English common law tradition, anyone detained by the state has a right to demand a hearing in front of a judge, in order to challenge the state's right to hold them, or, more literally, to have their body. Traditionally, habeas corpus rights were limited to a yes/no analysis: can the government detain this person? If yes, there was no subsequent, qualitative analysis about *how* exactly the body would be detained or treated. If no, then the person had to be released on the spot. So habeas corpus was a historically important, but fairly constrained right.

In 1791, when the Bill of Rights was ratified as the first ten amendments to the U.S. Constitution, convicted criminals got one more right: the Eighth Amendment protection against the infliction of cruel and unusual punishment. This right, too, was constrained. First, for those criminals convicted of state crimes, the Bill of Rights generally did not give individual citizens the ability to assert that their rights had been violated by state (as opposed to federal, or national) government officials. For instance, if a criminal in Massachusetts had a problem with the severity of the whipping he received as punishment in a Boston public square, he could only complain about this cruelty on the basis of rights he had under the Massachusetts constitution, in Massachusetts courts. Moreover, in 1791, when the Bill of Rights was ratified, prisons hardly existed. Instead of being incarcerated for a prescribed period of time, criminals were usually fined, whipped, or executed.

None of these punishments would have been considered either cruel or unusual.[24]

In the early 1800s, states began experimenting with prisons in place of public, corporal punishments. By the end of the nineteenth century, every state had a prison.[25] But prisoners' rights developed much more slowly. At first, anyone convicted of a crime and sentenced to prison in the United States was considered *civiliter mortuus*, or civilly dead. Being civilly dead means having no legal rights whatsoever: no rights to property, no rights to vote, and none of the other rights in the Bill of Rights. (Chapter Three further discusses the history and other aspects of civil death.) In fact, according to an infamous 1871 case in Virginia, prisoners became "slaves of the state."[26]

Woody Ruffin brought this 1871 Virginia case. He was imprisoned in Virginia, where prison officials hired him out to work as a convict laborer (essentially sold him into slavery), building a new railroad track. While at work one day, in the county of Bath, Ruffin killed one of the guards in an escape attempt. He was tried in front of a jury in nearby Richmond, Virginia, found guilty, and sentenced to hang. Ruffin argued that he should have been tried instead in Bath, the county where the murder took place. This was a technical legal argument, based on the Sixth Amendment right to a trial by jury in the district where a crime was committed. But the Virginia Supreme Court determined that, since Ruffin was a prisoner at the time of the murder, the Sixth Amendment right to a jury trial in the district where the crime was committed simply did not apply to him. Once imprisoned, then, a man could essentially be treated as if he were dead.

Often, in fact, prison did result in death, whether from overwork, lack of medical care, or execution. As Judge Thompson noted in the litigation around the use of the hitching post in Alabama, incarceration in

---

[24] See generally Lawrence Friedman, *Crime and Punishment in American History* (New York: Basic Books, 1994).

[25] Ashley T. Rubin, "A Neo-Institutional Account of Prison Diffusion," *Law and Society Review* 49, no. 2 (2015): 365–99; Michael Meranze, *Laboratories of Virtue: Punishment, Revolution, and Authority in Philadelphia, 1760–1835* (Chapel Hill: University of North Carolina Press, 1996).

[26] *Ruffin v. Commonwealth*, 62 Va. 790 (1871).

the nineteenth century was a dangerous proposition: prisoners working on chain gangs in the South after the Civil War, especially, died at "enormously high rates."

The concept of civil death lasted well into the twentieth century. In fact, as discussed in Chapters Three and Four, the concept arguably persists, in the form of ongoing twenty-first century limitations on prisoners' rights to regain their status as full citizens after a term of incarceration. But, beginning in the early 1950s, legal changes expanded civil rights for all kinds of marginalized groups, from women to African-Americans. These changes also shifted the landscape of prisoners' rights, laying the groundwork for prisoners like Larry Hope to challenge the conditions of their confinement.

First, beginning in 1953, federal courts expanded habeas corpus rights to include both a federal prisoner's ability to challenge the location and conditions of his confinement—as opposed to just the fact of his punishment—and a state prisoner's ability to bring a challenge in *federal* court to a *state* court's sentencing decision.[27] Then, in 1962 and 1963, the Supreme Court held that state prisoners prosecuted under state laws and punished by state officials could challenge the fact and terms of these state punishments in federal court, asserting that the state had violated their Eighth Amendment right to be free from cruel and unusual punishment.[28] This legal change was critical for someone like Larry Hope; state judges in Alabama were elected, and they tended to be unsympathetic to the claims of prisoners, who, incidentally, could not vote. Federal judges, by contrast, were appointed by the U.S. president, and tended to be more interested in enforcing consistent national standards, like the Eighth Amendment prohibition against cruel and unusual punishment.

In 1964, the U.S. Supreme Court provided yet a third way for prisoners to bring challenges to the conditions of their confinement in federal court: by asserting that their civil rights had been violated, under Section 1983 of the Civil Rights Act of 1871. These claims are often just called *Section 1983 claims*, and they usually concern unequal or inconsistent

---

[27] *Miller v. Overholser,* 206 F.2d 415 (D.C. Cir. 1953). *Brown v. Allen,* 344 U.S. 443 (1953).
[28] *Robinson v. California,* 370 U.S. 660 (1962); *Jones v. Cunningham,* 371 U.S. 236 (1963).

treatment. In *Cooper v. Pate*, the 1964 case that established this right, Thomas Cooper, a Muslim prisoner in Illinois, said he was being discriminated against on the basis of his religion: he was segregated from other prisoners, and he was refused access to a copy of the Quran. The federal district court in Illinois, as well as the Seventh Circuit appellate court, dismissed Cooper's claims, denying that he had such non-discrimination rights in prison. The U.S. Supreme Court disagreed, held that Cooper had "stated a cause of action," and ordered the lower courts to seriously evaluate Cooper's assertions about the rights violations he had experienced in Illinois prisons.[29] Ultimately, the district court ordered Illinois prison officials to permit Cooper to have a copy of the Quran and to participate in religious services.[30]

With the expansion of habeas rights, and the ability to bring both Eighth Amendment challenges and civil rights discrimination challenges against state prison officials, prisoners suddenly had a whole new litigation toolbox. And they used it. Prisoner lawsuits exploded. One of the first of these lawsuits concerned the brutal and inhumane conditions in Arkansas prisons (*Hutto v. Finney*); this case is discussed in further detail in Chapter Five.

Within two decades of the *Cooper* decision, as of 1981, there were eight thousand pending prisoner lawsuits challenging conditions of confinement and twenty-four states with either individual prisons or entire prison systems under court order to improve conditions of confinement.[31] If Larry Hope had brought his case against Alabama prison guards during this golden era of prison litigation, in the 1960s and 1970s, perhaps he would have been more successful.

By the mid-1980s, however, overwhelmed courts were establishing new rules to resist prisoner litigation. One of these new rules was the increasingly broad application of the qualified immunity doctrine, to

[29] *Cooper v. Pate*, 324 F.2d 165 (7th Cir. 1963), rev'd 378 U.S. 546 (1964).

[30] *Cooper v. Pate*, 382 F.2d 518 (7th Cir. 1967).

[31] *Rhodes v. Chapman*, 452 U.S. 337 (1981); Malcolm Feeley and Edward Rubin, *Judicial Policy Making and the Modern State: How the Courts Reformed America's Prisons* (New York: Cambridge University Press, 2000).

defend prison guards against suits by prisoners, as in Larry Hope's case.[32] Subsequent rules included the establishment of the deliberate indifference standard, which put the burden on prisoners like Hope to prove that prison officials both (1) knew about and (2) purposefully ignored a dangerous situation.[33] Of course, proving what someone else knew and intended is hard to do in any circumstance, let alone from the relatively powerless position of a prisoner. As Larry Hope learned first-hand, both the qualified immunity doctrine, protecting prison guards from liability, and the deliberate indifference standard, requiring firm proof of what prison guards knew and intended, made prisoner lawsuits much harder to initiate and to win.

Logistically, the increasing limitations on prisoners' rights were fortuitously timed. Not only were prisoner lawsuits burgeoning, but the prison population itself was expanding quickly. Courts could barely handle all the prisoner litigation they were facing in the 1980s, as the U.S. prison population began its exponential climb. What would happen as prison populations increased?

THE PEANUT BUTTER CASE
AND RIGHTS LIMITATIONS

In the 1990s, the question of how to limit prison litigation got politicized. It all started in Arizona, where the state Department of Corrections had faced decades of litigation over its prisoner mail regulations. Starting in 1973, as prisoners were exercising their new rights to challenge their conditions of confinement all over the United States, Arizona prisoners filed a class action lawsuit complaining about prison policies that severely limited the mail they could send and receive. These limitations, the prisoners argued, violated their First Amendment rights to freedom of speech and to petition the government for redress of grievances. (U.S. federal courts

---

[32] *Cleavinger v. Saxner,* 474 U.S. 193 (1985); Michael C. Dorf, "Supreme Court Jail Suicide Case Illustrates the Breadth of Qualified Immunity," *Verdict: Justia,* Jun. 3, 2015, https://verdict.justia.com/2015/06/03/supreme-court-jail-suicide-case-illustrates-the-breadth-of-qualified-immunity.

[33] *Farmer v. Brennan,* 511 U.S. 825 (1994); Dolovich, "Forms of Deference."

have held that prisoners have at least limited First Amendment rights.) Within a year, prison officials agreed to a *consent decree*—a settlement in which they promised to revise the mail regulations, but admitted no liability for prior constitutional violations.

But in the 1990s, prisoners started to complain that prison officials were ignoring the promises made in that 1973 consent decree. Judge Carl Muecke, who had heard the original complaints, agreed. He appointed a *special master*—an independent investigator who would look into allegations of noncompliance with the original consent decree and monitor enforcement of the mail regulations.[34]

At this point, Arizona politicians were enraged. The governor, Fife Symington, conducted a public relations campaign against the lawsuit and the federal judge overseeing it. Symington issued press releases and wrote extended letters to local papers, complaining about how Judge Muecke had cost the state millions of dollars of legal costs and monitoring fees, all to guarantee that "murderers" and "rapists" were comfortable in prison and even had access to sexually explicit materials.[35] (Muecke had established his liberal reputation decades earlier, ordering the desegregation of Arizona schools one year before the U.S. Supreme Court mandated national desegregation in *Brown v. Board of Education*.[36]) But Symington also worked with legislators, in Arizona and at the federal level in Washington, D.C., to translate his outrage into legal limitations on prisoner litigation and judicial intervention. In particular, he collaborated with Senator John Kyl, an Arizona Republican, to introduce the Prison Litigation Reform Act (PLRA) in Congress, in 1995.

The PLRA proposed a number of limitations on prisoner litigation: caps to the rates attorneys could bill for representing prisoners and caps to the costs judges could incur in ordering monitoring of prisons; procedural restrictions on the kinds of claims prisoners could raise in

[34] *Hook v. Arizona*, 972 F.2d 1012 (9th Cir. 1992).

[35] Mona Lynch, *Sunbelt Justice: Arizona and the Transformation of American Punishment* (Stanford: Stanford University Press, 2009), 188–191.

[36] "Obituaries: Carl Muecke, 89; Retired U.S. Judge Was Guided by His Liberal Convictions," *Los Angeles Times*, Sept. 25, 2007, http://articles.latimes.com/2007/sep/25/local/me-muecke25.

challenging prison conditions; and prohibitions against prisoners who file "frivolous" lawsuits having their claims heard in federal court.[37] Robert Dole of Kansas, another Republican senator, explained why he supported Senator Kyl's legislation:

> Let me be more specific. According the Arizona attorney general Grant Woods, a staggering 45 percent of the civil cases filed in Arizona's Federal courts last year were filed by state prisoners. That means that 20,000 prisoners in Arizona filed almost as many cases as Arizona's 3.5 million law-abiding citizens. And most of these prisoner lawsuits were filed free of charge. No court costs. No filing fees. This is outrageous and it must stop.[38]

Symington, Kyl, and Dole were concerned with the number of lawsuits being filed and the injustice of people who had broken laws being permitted to file such suits—at a reduced cost, no less. But they were also concerned with the filing of "frivolous" lawsuits. Dole described prisoner suits complaining about "the failure of prison officials to invite a prisoner to a pizza party for a departing prison employee," and suits complaining about "being served chunky peanut butter instead of the creamy variety."[39] The "Peanut Butter Case" became the sound bite that sold the PLRA. The law passed in 1996.

But Senator Dole had misrepresented the entire premise of the Peanut Butter Case. The prisoner who brought that case was not complaining about the kind of peanut butter he got. He was complaining about the fact that his prison commissary account was never credited for the cost of the jar of peanut butter he returned. The amount missing was $2.50.[40]

---

[37] Lynch, *Sunbelt Justice*; Margo Schlanger, "Civil Rights Injunctions over Time: A Case Study of Jail and Prison Court Orders," *New York University Law Review* 81 (2006): 550–630.

[38] Robert Dole, "Hearings on 'Prisoner Litigation Reform Act,'" Congressional Record, September 27, 1995, quoted online here: http://jthomasniu.org/class/Papers/prisdrew.txt.

[39] Ibid.

[40] Jon O. Newman, "Not All Prisoner Lawsuits are Frivolous," *Prison Legal News*, Apr. 1996: 6, https://www.prisonlegalnews.org/news/1996/apr/15/not-all-prisoner-lawsuits-are-frivolous/.

That might sound like nothing to you or me. But to a prisoner, whose *daily* wage might be $1 or $2—if he is lucky enough to have a job in prison— $2.50 represents a few days' wages.[41] Hence the validity of the Peanut Butter Case claim. And as other critics of Dole's hyperbole have pointed out, the senator conveniently failed to mention the dozens of legitimate lawsuits brought by prisoners across the United States in the 1970s and 1980s, alleging they had been electrocuted, whipped, isolated; denied food, healthcare, mail, and visits; and subjected to living with raw sewage.[42] The Peanut Butter Case and electrocutions represent two extremes of prison litigation. But as noted above in Larry Hope's case, the vast majority of prisoner litigation before (and after) passage of the Prison Litigation Reform Act has concerned potentially serious, often life-threatening issues. Nonetheless, the idea of the Peanut Butter Case resonated.

After its passage in 1996, the PLRA did, indeed, stop the barrage of prisoner litigation. The rate of prisoner civil rights cases filed in federal district courts fell from a peak of 25 per 1,000 prisoners in 1995, to less than half that in 1998, just two years after the passage of PLRA: 12 per 1,000 prisoners. By 2006, the rate of filings was less than 10 cases per 1,000 prisoners. Even though the raw number of people incarcerated increased steadily over this period, from just over 1.6 million in 1996 to 2.3 million in 2006, the raw number of civil rights cases filed by prisoners decreased steadily, from roughly 38,000 in 1996 to 22,000 in 2006.[43]

After qualified immunity, deliberate indifference, and the Prison Litigation Reform Act, what rights remain for prisoners? By the time Larry Hope was trying to hold prison officials accountable for chaining him to the hitching post, he was not only facing the procedural challenges of overcoming qualified immunity and proving deliberate indifference; now, he also encountered the roadblock of the PLRA. The PLRA prevented any

[41] Peter Wagner, *The Prison Index: Taking the Pulse of the Crime Control Industry* (Northampton: Western Prison Project and Prison Policy Initiative, Apr. 2003), http://www .prisonpolicy.org/prisonindex/prisonlabor.html.

[42] Mark Tushnet and Larry Yackle, "Symbolic Statutes and Real Laws: The Pathologies of the Antiterrorism and Effective Death Penalty Act and the Prison Litigation Reform Act," *Duke Law Journal* 47, no. 1 (1997): 1–86, at 64.

[43] Margo Schlanger, "Trends in Prison Litigation, as the PLRA Enters Adulthood," *UC Irvine Law Review* 5 (2015): 153–78, Table 1.

lawyer willing to represent Hope from charging more than 150 percent of the rate paid to publicly appointed defense counsel, usually well under the average hourly wage for civil rights litigation.[44] The PLRA required Hope to file internal administrative grievances with prison officials at Limestone Correctional Facility before he could even seek permission to file a claim in federal court.[45] And the PLRA limited the relief that any court could grant Hope or fellow class members.

With early civil rights cases in the 1960s, like *Cooper v. Pate*, courts essentially raised prisoners from the dead (or at least released them from the status of *civiliter mortuus*) and gave them the ability to assert their First and Eighth Amendment rights, civil rights, and rights to be heard in court: at all. But then, over the course of the 1980s and 1990s, these rights were slowly constrained, raising a central question: today, can any prisoner ever hope to establish the existence of a constitutional violation in prison, let alone win relief—either in terms of a new policy or a payment of damages?

---

[44] Assessing the actual costs—and benefits—of prison litigation is difficult. Costs include the fees paid to prisoners' lawyers, the time state lawyers and judges spend defending and adjudicating these cases, fees paid to experts and monitors, damages fees paid to prisoners, and the infrastructure and staffing costs of implementing remedies like providing more up-to-date physical facilities, or adequate healthcare. In a class action case, these costs can be in the millions, or even billions. But the benefits—beyond improved care, conditions, or rights enforcement—can also be significant and include reducing the high medical costs associated with untreated illnesses; reducing violence or recidivism through low-cost, early interventions; or even reducing the overall prison operating costs through prison population reductions. For a cost-benefit analysis of one particular class action case around prison conditions in Pennsylvania, see Sarah Vandenbraak Hart, "Evaluating Institutional Prisoners' Rights Litigation: Costs and Benefits and Federalism Considerations," *Journal of Constitutional Law* 11, no. 1 (2008): 73–100, http://scholarship.law.upenn.edu/cgi/viewcontent.cgi?article=1143&context=jcl.

[45] The grievance systems required by the PLRA have been controversial. Some scholars argue that grievance requirements provide a streamlined process and institutional accountability facilitating resolution of prisoner problems quickly, within facilities. Others argue that grievance requirements force prisoners to scramble to meet unreasonable timelines in making complaints and tend to provide cursory and dismissive answers to these complaints, creating yet another hurdle that prisoners must overcome before asserting their rights in court. For a socio-legal analysis of the history and implementation of grievance policies in California prisons, see Kitty Calavita and Valerie Jenness, *Appealing to Justice: Prisoner Grievances, Rights, and Carceral Logic* (Berkeley: University of California Press, 2014).

WHAT RIGHTS ARE LEFT?

Amazingly, in spite of the roadblocks, prisoners like Larry Hope still manage to file, litigate, and even sometimes win challenges to the conditions of their confinement. Although the Prison Litigation Reform Act did reduce prisoner litigation, the act has not even come close to eliminating prisoners' suits. As the statistics presented above suggest, tens of thousands of prisoners each year do file cases challenging prison conditions. Roughly ten percent of these prisoner plaintiffs actually win some relief.[46]

In states with strong legal advocacy communities, or independent oversight bodies, litigation has remained especially robust. For instance, California has a nonprofit law firm, the Prison Law Office, which has independently litigated dozens of class action cases on behalf of state prisoners, winning a number of cases to improve conditions of confinement. New York and Illinois both have independent monitoring organizations—the Correctional Association of New York and the John Howard Association of Illinois—with state mandates allowing them to visit prisons and monitor conditions, and each has facilitated litigation and conditions reform. Illinois also has the Uptown People's Law Center, which functions something like the Prison Law Office, representing individuals and classes of prisoners in civil rights cases. In each of these states, litigation has at least kept the pressure on prison systems to remain somewhat transparent and to justify deviations from and exceptions to constitutionally guaranteed rights.

In recent years, litigation in California has been unusually successful in terms of both establishing egregious constitutional violations and achieving litigation-based remedies to those violations. One case attracted national attention in 2011, when the U.S. Supreme Court agreed to hear an appeal brought by the state of California. Governor Jerry Brown objected to a lower court order to release tens of thousands of state prisoners, to remedy unconstitutionally overcrowded prison conditions. Not only did the U.S. Supreme Court agree to hear the prisoners' rights case, the Court

[46] Schlanger, "Trends."

then upheld the prisoner release order. This was shocking, as prison legal scholar Margo Schlanger pointed out in the aftermath:

> Not since 1978 had the Court ratified a lower court's crowding-related order in a jail or prison case, and the order before the Court in 2011 was fairly aggressive; theoretically, it could have (although this was never a real prospect) induced the release of tens of thousands of sentenced prisoners or the expenditure of billions of dollars in new prison construction.[47]

Justice Scalia, known as a colorfully conservative justice, in his dissent in this case, echoed Schlanger's surprise: "Today the Court affirms what is perhaps the most radical injunction issued by a court in our Nation's history: an order requiring California to release the staggering number of 46,000 convicted criminals."[48]

What exactly was going on in California that so many federal judges were in agreement that thousands of prisoners had to be released? It all started with Marciano Plata, as described in a petition filed in a federal district court in Northern California in 2001. Plata injured his knee in the 1990s. The injury was so bad that Plata frequently had difficulty walking. He complained to prison doctors, but they refused to provide the necessary surgery for the injury, and they refused to excuse him from work. He struggled to walk, and to work. He kept falling and injuring his head. Finally, after two years, he received the surgery he needed. Immediately following his surgery, prison officials discharged Plata from the hospital infirmary and left him to walk on his own back to his housing unit—no brace, crutches, or other mobility assistance provided. To make matters worse, Plata had difficulty understanding English, but prison officials refused to provide translators for him at medical appointments.[49]

The persistent callousness of the treatment Plata received built a strong case for overcoming qualified immunity and establishing deliberate

[47] Margo Schlanger, "*Plata v. Brown* and Realignment: Jails, Prisons, Courts, and Politics," *Harvard Civil Rights and Civil Liberties Law Review* 48, no. 1 (2013): 165–215.

[48] *Plata v. Brown*, 563 U.S. 493 (2011).

[49] *Plata v. Davis* Complaint, No. 01-CV-01351-TEH (N.D. Cal. 2001): 2–4.

indifference—hurdles Larry Hope had struggled to clear. Even more importantly, Marciano Plata was far from alone. The original complaint in the *Plata* case was brimming with stories like Plata's: a prisoner who received no wound care following an operation to place a dialysis shunt; a patient with AIDS who suffered eight bouts of severe withdrawal from sporadically administered doses of methadone (for pain); and a paraplegic prisoner who was refused treatment for urinary tract infections for months. Over the course of litigation in the *Plata* case, lawyers for the prisoners collected enough of these stories of egregious lapses in the provision of basic healthcare to establish that one prisoner per week was dying "needlessly" in California prisons.[50] Fifty-two prisoners per year, dead, for lack of access to basic healthcare, all while they lived in one of the ten richest countries in the world, in a state that itself ranked as the sixth largest economy in the world. How could this happen?

At first, the federal court in California overseeing the case ordered improvements to medical care, appointed experts to monitor state prisons, and insisted that the state invest more money in hiring doctors and providing healthcare. But the problems persisted. By 2006, the *Plata* case had been in litigation for five years, and conditions hardly seemed to be improving. Prisoners were still dying, and the prisons just seemed to get more overcrowded. And costs were skyrocketing. The state had spent millions in litigation, paying state monitors, and hiring additional medical staff. So the prisoners' lawyers sought a "population reduction order." They argued that the only way to solve the problems with unconstitutional healthcare in California prisons was to reduce the number of people in prison who needed healthcare.

A "population reduction order" was a remedy that the 1996 Prison Litigation Reform Act permitted, if a specially convened panel of three federal judges ordered the reduction. When Prison Law Office lawyers requested the population reduction order, the request triggered the formation of the three-judge panel. More litigation ensued. Then-Attorney General Jerry Brown—who had been governor of California from 1973 to 1985 and was

---

[50] As characterized by Justice Kennedy in the *Plata* decision. *Plata v. Brown*, 563 U.S. 493 (2011).

soon-to-be re-elected governor in 2011—resisted the claim that population overcrowding was causing the constitutionally inadequate medical care in the state prisons.[51] The judges disagreed.

In 2009, there were 171,275 people in prison in California—more than in any other U.S. state, and more than in all but nine other nations.[52] Perhaps unsurprisingly, there simply were not enough beds in California prisons for all these prisoners. The prison system was functioning at or above 200 percent of its designed capacity. When the Supreme Court issued an opinion in the case two years later, they included pictures— a first in a Supreme Court opinion—of beds stacked three-high, lined up, row after row, in hallways, gyms, and any open space in any given prison.[53] This extreme overcrowding made every aspect of managing life in California prisons—from offering educational or treatment programs, to controlling violence, to providing basic healthcare—extremely difficult for guards and staff working in state prison facilities.

The lack of healthcare in California prisons, then, was not just a result of official callousness or indifference; it was also a result of the large number of people in prisons in the state—numbers over which prison officials themselves had little control. Punishment scholars have described how even the most well-intentioned prison officials and reformers must balance conscience, or doing the right thing, against convenience, or doing the expedient thing.[54] Providing adequate healthcare to so many prisoners turned out to be not only inconvenient, but nearly impossible.

The federal judges trying to keep one prisoner a week from dying decided that the only way this would be possible would be to reduce the

[51] Keramet Reiter and Natalie Pifer, "Brown v. Plata," Oxford Handbook of Crime and Criminal Justice, Michael Tonry, ed. (New York: Oxford University Press, 2011). DOI: 10.1093/oxfordhb/9780199935383.013.113.

[52] Ann Carson and William J. Sabol, Prisoners in 2011, Washington, D.C.: US Department of Justice, Bureau of Justice Statistics, 2012, http://www.bjs.gov/content/pub/pdf/p11. pdf; International Center for Prison Studies, "Highest to Lowest Prison Population Total," 2014, http://www.prisonstudies.org/highest-to-lowest/prison-population-otal? field_regio n_taxo no my_tid=All.

[53] See Plata v. Brown, 563 U.S. 493 (2011).

[54] For a classic analysis of this argument, see David J. Rothman, Conscience and Convenience: The Asylum and Its Alternatives in Progressive America (Boston: Little Brown & Co., 1980).

prison population. They ordered California officials to figure out how to get the prison population down to 137.5 percent of "design capacity," which would, at least, be less seriously overcrowded. Attorney General Brown appealed this order to the Supreme Court.[55]

When the Supreme Court upheld the population reduction order, prisoners' rights advocates celebrated. Punishment scholar Jonathan Simon published a book arguing that the *Plata* case had finally put *Mass Incarceration on Trial* in the United States. And mass incarceration, Simon argued, had lost. Simon emphasized the important role of dignity in the Supreme Court's decision.[56] Justice Kennedy, one of the Supreme Court justices especially concerned with international human rights principles, wrote the majority opinion supporting the population reduction order in the *Plata* case. Kennedy argued that the Eighth Amendment prohibition against cruel and unusual punishment embodied a concept of "human dignity," which had been violated in California.[57] Simon, in turn, argued that this emphasis on dignity provided an escape route from mass incarceration: prioritizing prisoners' humanity requires de-prioritizing their criminality.[58] More immediately, focusing on human dignity implies a more robust way of thinking about prisoners' rights and, perhaps, overcoming limitations to exercising those rights, like qualified immunity and deliberate indifference.

The aftermath of the *Plata* decision, however, reveals that both rolling back mass incarceration and rethinking limitations on prisoners' basic rights are complex processes. Following the Supreme Court's decision in *Plata*, lawyers, legislators, and judges worked together to reach agreement on how to remedy the state's overcrowding problem. Would they release prisoners? Would they build more prisons? In the end, they decided to punt the decision to each of California's fifty-eight counties. The

---

[55] See Reiter and Pifer, *"Brown v. Plata."*

[56] Jonathan Simon, *Mass Incarceration on Trial: A Remarkable Court Decision and the Future of Prisons in America* (New York: New Press, 2014).

[57] *Plata v. Brown*, 563 U.S. 493 (2011).

[58] Ferguson also discusses this tension in his book *Inferno*, highlighting the ideological contradictions between humanity and criminality. Robert A. Ferguson, *Inferno: An Anatomy of American Punishment* (Cambridge, MA: Harvard University Press, 2014).

legislature passed a law called the "Criminal Justice Realignment Act of 2011," known informally just as "Realignment." The law shifted certain categories of nonserious, nonviolent, non-sex-offender-registry-eligible offenders ("non-non-nons" or "triple-nons") from state prisons into county facilities. Counties could then decide whether to find local jail space, halfway-house space, or other resources for these non-non-nons. Some county jails quickly became overcrowded, violent, and under-resourced. Within a year of the Supreme Court's decision in *Plata*, some of the bigger county jails, like the jail in Fresno, faced exactly the same problems California state prisons had faced prior to the *Plata* litigation and the implementation of Realignment. Prison Law Office lawyers noticed and brought new litigation to challenge conditions in these local jail facilities, prompting legal scholars to comment that California's prison overcrowding problems resembled a "hydra"—a mythical creature with multiple snake heads that just grow back as soon as they are cut off.[59]

State prison systems, like California's department of corrections, are centralized under a director of corrections, who usually reports directly to a state governor and legislature. This centralization means that an entire state prison system can be subject to one overarching court order, as in the *Plata* case. But cities and counties run jails, so each jail facility must be separately sued, and court orders for reform can only be obtained one at a time. Unconstitutional conditions in jails, then, present especially difficult challenges to oversight bodies like the Prison Law Office, or the federal Department of Justice, which also investigates unconstitutional conditions in prisons and jails across the United States.[60] Although the idea of dignity might have justified a reduction in California's state prison population, the problems with overcrowding and unconstitutional conditions just shifted down to the counties, where prisoners and their

[59] Schlanger, "*Plata v. Brown* and Realignment"; Reiter and Pifer, "*Brown v. Plata*."
[60] For a succinct description of the challenges of conditions of confinement litigation in jails, see Alysia Santo, "When an Old Law Makes It Hard to Fix a Troubled Jail," *The Marshall Project*, Sept. 13, 2016, https://www.themarshallproject.org/2016/09/13/when-an-old-law-makes-it-hard-to-fix-a-troubled-jail?utm_medium=email&utm_campaign=newsletter&utm_source=opening-statement&utm_term=newsletter-20160914-584#.TZ1W49P5K.

advocates started the process all over again of gathering stories of abuse, working to overcome claims of qualified immunity, and attempting to establish evidence of deliberate indifference.

Meanwhile, however, prisoners in one particular California prison in the northernmost corner of the state capitalized on all the attention California prisons were receiving in the early 2010s about unconstitutional conditions of confinement. Instead of a simple lack of adequate healthcare, these prisoners complained about a lack of any resources at all. They were in long-term solitary confinement, locked alone in windowless eight-by-ten-foot poured cement cells, in the Pelican Bay Security Housing Unit (SHU) in Crescent City, California, near the state's border with Oregon. In the SHU, prisoners had no access to phones, people, or daily activities of any kind, and healthcare was scarce, too.

In July of 2011, prisoners in long-term solitary confinement in the Pelican Bay SHU began to refuse food. Over the next few weeks, more than six thousand prisoners across the state refused food in solidarity with those in the SHU. The hunger-striking prisoners demanded basic improvements in the conditions of solitary confinement: the provision of adequate and nutritious food, the right to have a photograph taken once a year and sent to their families, the right to have warm clothes to wear for their hour per day in a solitary exercise yard.[61]

The prisoners also demanded greater *procedural protections* with which to defend themselves from being placed in solitary confinement. Each of the prisoners leading the strike had been "validated" as a gang member and sent to isolation for an indefinite period of time—usually presumptively for the duration of his prison sentence. Prison officials (not judges or juries) determined whether prisoners qualified for validation as gang members. Validation was simple: prison officials only had to collect three pieces of evidence of gang association. "Evidence" could be as informal and as tangential as having a tattoo (for instance, an inked Aztec symbol might establish Mexican Mafia membership) or being in possession of revolutionary literature (for instance, George Jackson's bestselling book

---

[61] For details about the history and goals of the strike, see generally the following website: https://prisonerhungerstrikesolidarity.wordpress.com.

Soledad Brother might establish Black Guerilla Family membership).[62] Prison officials conducted this validation process in short hearings at which prisoners had no right to a lawyer, or even to see the evidence used to establish their gang membership.

As it turned out, this validation process had decades-long implications for prisoners. During the July 2011 hunger strike, journalists requested information from the California prison system about how many prisoners had been in isolation for how long. Prison officials revealed that more than five hundred prisoners had each been in total solitary confinement in the Pelican Bay SHU for more than ten years.[63] (Chapter Two discusses the psychological implications of such conditions of confinement in detail.) The strike attracted national and international attention; Amnesty International visited the Pelican Bay SHU and condemned the conditions there as "cruel, inhuman, and degrading," in violation of international law.[64] As the hunger strikers entered a dangerous third week without food, California prison officials sat down with the strike leaders in a small office at the Pelican Bay prison, to discuss their demands. Prison officials agreed to some small concessions: allowing prisoners to have that one photo a year, warm hats, and colored pencils for drawing.[65] Prison officials also initiated other reforms behind the scenes, including the elimination of automatic assignment of anyone validated as a gang member to indefinite isolation, in places like the Pelican Bay SHU.[66]

[62] Keramet Reiter, "(Un)settling Solitary Confinement in California," *Social Justice*, Sept. 28, http://www.socialjusticejournal.org/?p=3214.

[63] Julie Small, "Under Scrutiny, Pelican Bay Prison Officials Say They Target Only Gang Leaders," *KPCC radio* [Pasadena, California], Aug. 23, 2011, www.scpr.org/news/2011/08/23/28382/pelican-bay-prison-officials-say-they-lock-gang-bo.

[64] *USA: The Edge of Endurance—Prison Conditions in California's Security Housing Units*, (London: Amnesty International, 2012), http://www.amnestyusa.org/sites/default/files/edgeofendurancecaliforniareport.pdf.

[65] Keramet Reiter, "The Pelican Bay Hunger Strike: Resistance Within the Structural Constraints of a U.S. Supermax Prison," *South Atlantic Quarterly* 113, no. 3 (Summer 2014): 579–611.

[66] California Department of Corrections and Rehabilitation, "CDCR's Response to Hunger Striker's Demands," *CDCR Today,* Aug. 26, 2013, http://cdcrtoday.blogspot.com/2013/08/cdcrs-responses-to-hunger-strikers.html.

Prisoners, however, remained frustrated with the slow place of reforms. They coordinated two more hunger strikes. An unprecedented 30,000 prisoners participated over almost sixty days in the third strike in 2013. The prisoners also pursued a lawsuit. They sought to prove to a federal judge that their rights had been violated. Unlike Larry Hope, the Pelican Bay SHU prisoners did not demand damages for their injuries. Instead, the SHU prisoners demanded changes to prison policies: the abolition of the gang validation process and the elimination of indefinite isolation terms. Because they sought policy changes (or *injunctive relief*) rather than damages, the SHU prisoners did not have to name specific individuals who had harmed them, or overcome qualified immunity. Still, to win court-ordered reforms, the prisoners would have to prove that their Eighth Amendment rights had been violated. Even before that, the SHU prisoners had to establish that they were a *class*, with shared interests and similar claims, such that a judge could hear all the cases together and address the common complaints with one remedy.

In June of 2014, federal Judge Claudia Wilken, in Oakland, California, *certified the class* of the five hundred prisoners who had been in the Pelican Bay SHU for ten years or more.[67] Class certification signaled that Judge Wilken thought the prisoners had valid claims, which deserved to be heard in court. Just nine months later, the prisoners and their lawyers filed ten expert reports, each focusing on describing in grim detail the destructive impact of long-term solitary confinement on: psychological well-being, physical health, and even institutional safety and security.[68] Facing down the public critique from organizations like Amnesty International, and the powerful evidence levied in the litigation on behalf of the SHU prisoners, California prison officials began to talk with the prisoners and their lawyers about settling the case.

One year later, the case finally did settle. Prison officials agreed to abandon nearly all of the practices about which the hunger-striking prisoners had complained. Only prisoners who broke specific in-prison rules

[67] "*Ashker v. Governor of California*," Center for Constitutional Rights, https://ccrjustice.org/home/what-we-do/our-cases/ashker-v-brown.
[68] "Expert Reports in *Ashker v. Brown*," Center for Constitutional Rights, Aug. 3, 2015, https://ccrjustice.org/expert-reports-ashker-v-brown.

(and not merely validated gang members) would be sent into isolation. Five years would be the new, hard limit on the length of any term in isolation. All the changes would apply retroactively, so every member of that class of prisoners certified by Judge Wilken would be removed from isolation, within one year.[69] One year after the settlement, in the summer of 2016, the 1,056-bed long-term solitary confinement unit at Pelican Bay State Prison had only a few hundred prisoners left in it.[70] Together, the hunger striking prisoners had been able to overcome many of the challenges prisoners have historically faced to bringing and winning legal cases to assert—and enforce—their rights.

---

[69] "Summary of *Ashker v. Governor of California* Settlement Terms," Center for Constitutional Rights, Sept. 1, 2015, https://ccrjustice.org/sites/default/files/attach/2015/08/2015-09-01-Ashker-settlement-summary.pdf.

[70] Alex Emslie, "A Year After Settlement, Hundreds of State Prison Isolation Cells Empty," KQED: *The California Report*, Sept. 4, 2016, https://ww2.kqed.org/news/2016/09/04/a-year-after-settlement-hundreds-of-state-prison-isolation-cells-empty/.

[2]

THE PRISON WITHIN THE PRISON: MENTAL ILLNESS AND PUNITIVE TOOLS OF CONTROL

In August of 2013, Joseph Duran received a seven-year sentence for a robbery he had committed in Southern California. He was transferred from *jail*, where people are held before they have been tried and sentenced, or if they are serving out sentences of less than one year, to state *prison*, where people are sent once they have received a sentence of one year or more.[1] Duran was thirty-four and familiar with prison. He had been born to drug-addicted parents, removed from their home, and adopted at the age of five. But he himself turned to drug use as a teenager, suffered from serious mental illness, and seemed always to be in confrontations with authority figures. In 2006, he got in a fight with police, which ended in the placement of a tracheotomy tube in his throat. As soon as he arrived at California's North Kern State Prison in August of 2013, Duran got in trouble for assaulting a guard. Then he started talking about suicide. Prison officials quickly transferred him to a "mental health crisis bed," essentially a solitary confinement cell under frequent surveillance, at Mule Creek State Prison, two-hundred-odd miles north of North Kern State Prison.[2]

---

[1] "Fact Detail: What is the Difference Between Jails and Prisons?" Bureau of Justice Statistics, Department of Justice, http://www.bjs.gov/index.cfm?ty=qa&iid=322. In California, the jail-prison distinction has recently been blurred. Post the Realignment policies that followed the *Plata* decision, as discussed in Chapter One, some nonviolent prisoners (the "non-non-nons" previously discussed) are actually being held in local jails, even though they have been sentenced to more than one year in prison.

[2] Sam Stanton and Denny Walsh, "$750,000 settlement reached in death of inmate pepper sprayed in the face," *Sacramento Bee*, Aug. 22, 2016, http://www.sacbee.com/news/local/crime/article97246522.html#storylink=cpy.

This was two years after the Supreme Court's decision in the *Plata* case, which had ordered significant reductions in the state's prison population, in an effort to make providing constitutionally adequate healthcare to prisoners more feasible. Over the course of the *Plata* litigation, the state prison population decreased steadily. Between 2009 and 2013, it fell by one-quarter, from a peak of over 170,000 prisoners in 2009 to 120,000 prisoners in August of 2013, when Joseph Duran landed in prison.[3] And the rate of unnecessary prisoner deaths—the shocking statistic of one per week that had been noted in the Supreme Court's *Plata* decision—had fallen dramatically, too. Duran's quick transfer to a prison that could meet his obvious mental health needs seemed like exactly the kind of action courts had hoped to institutionalize throughout the *Plata* litigation. But then things started to go wrong—both for Duran and for California prison officials' attempts to prove they no longer required close judicial scrutiny to prevent unnecessary deaths.

This chapter begins with the story of Joseph Duran's death, then works backward to detail the mid-twentieth-century political reforms that moved prisoners like Duran out of hospital settings and into carceral settings. The chapter next examines the tools—most notably solitary confinement—that prison officials have developed to manage (and mismanage) the mentally ill, and finally concludes by exploring the ethical conundrum of how people working in prisons negotiate their obligations to both punish and protect.

Whereas prisoners like Larry Hope had to organize to overcome multiple procedural hurdles in order to bring prison abuses to light and seek improvements in conditions, prisoners like Joseph Duran must rely on both the compassion of individual caretakers and the ethical functioning of institutions of social control to survive, let alone to have their stories told. Throughout, this chapter examines both individual obligations—between prison staff and prisoners—and institutional

[3] Ryken Grattet and Joseph Hayes, "Just the Facts: California's Changing Prison Population," *Prison Policy*, Apr. 2015, http://www.ppic.org/content/pubs/jtf/JTF_PrisonsJTF.pdf. See also Ann Carson and William J. Sabol, *Prisoners in 2011*, Washington, D.C.: U.S. Department of Justice, Bureau of Justice Statistics, 2012, http://www.bjs.gov/content/pub/pdf/p11.pdf.

obligations—within prisons, hospitals, courts, and the media. Consider not only how these obligations play out in these stories, but how they should play out under ideal laws and policies.

JOSEPH DURAN

When he arrived at Mule Creek, on September 4, 2013, the day after his thirty-fifth birthday, prison staff placed Duran in a cell by himself, on suicide watch. At Mule Creek, Duran would have had little time outside of his cell on any given day, and little contact with other prisoners; he was in solitary confinement, albeit for his own protection. Because he was on suicide watch, someone had to look inside his cell every fifteen minutes. At Mule Creek, Duran refused to take medications. He also refused to eat. He claimed he was being poisoned.

At 3:30 p.m. on September 6, a prison psychiatrist recommended involuntary medication. But a few hours later, against healthcare recommendations, prison officials removed Duran's suicide watch status. At 10:30 that evening, Duran pressed his face into the open "food port" in his cell door—a slot, just about at waist level, through which officers slide food trays into a prisoner's cell at mealtimes. Probably, guards had opened the port to see into the cell as they conducted a "count" to make sure every prisoner was in his cell. By pressing his face against the port, or grabbing on, Duran kept the guards from closing the port and sealing off his cell. Guards ordered him to move back. He refused. So officer Roy C. Chavez blasted him with pepper spray, drenching Duran's face and neck. Duran moved away from the food port. Officer Chavez closed the port and left him alone.[4]

Pepper spray is, more precisely, a "lachrymatory agent," or a variety of tear gas. Pepper spray is "natural" in that it is actually made from a concentrated version of the chemical in chili peppers (as opposed to tear gas, which contains man-made chemical compounds). People who have

[4] Sam Stanton and Denny Walsh, "Was It Suicide? Questions Abound in Death of Pepper-Sprayed Inmate," *Sacramento Bee*, Jan. 21, 2014, http://www.sacbee.com/news/investigations/the-public-eye/article2589344.html. Video-taped news coverage available here: https://www.youtube.com/watch?v=EhfBuNwNmuU.

experienced both tear gas and pepper spray say that pepper spray is more painful. It can cause temporary blindness, intense coughing, and burning of the skin. The effect is especially intense on mucous membranes, like in nostrils and throats. Pepper spray is oil-based, so it cannot be rubbed or washed off; its acute effects can last as long as fifteen minutes, and the burning sensations can linger for hours.[5] Although "pepper spray" is a fairly literal term for the active ingredient in the spray (capsaicin), some have argued that the term actually "helps to cloak abuses of authority by making tear gas sound like a condiment."[6]

After he was doused in pepper spray, and sealed into his cell alone, with limited ventilation, Duran began to experience an intense burning sensation in his eyes, throat, and skin. Because the burning is worst on mucous membranes, Duran likely would have experienced horrible burning especially around his tracheal tube, where mucous membranes would have been exposed. This probably explains why he tore his tracheal tube out of his throat, started coughing up blood, and stuffed spaghetti from his dinner plate into the gaping hole in his neck.[7] Using spaghetti was not a horrible way to try to mitigate the burning sensation; rice or pasta might cut the burn of chili peppers in cooking, and home remedies for minimizing pepper spray pain including coating affected areas with whole milk (which Duran probably did not have available to him).

Next ensued a standoff between the prison guards, whom Duran had been antagonizing, and the doctors, who could have helped to alleviate his suffering. Notes from prison files reveal that, two hours after Officer Chavez pepper sprayed Duran, a prison doctor ordered Duran removed from his cell, so that he could be "decontaminated" of the pepper spray, "medicated," and have his tracheal tube reinserted into his throat. Prison guards refused. They said Duran was "too dangerous to move." Every few hours, medical

---

[5] Jessica Smith, "What Is the Difference Between Pepper Spray and Tear Gas?" *Berkeley Science Review*, 2012, http://berkeleysciencereview.com/what-is-the-difference-between-pepper-spray-and-tear-gas/.

[6] Keramet Reiter and Thomas Blair, "Punishing Mental Illness: Transinstitutionalization and Solitary Confinement in the United States," in *Extreme Punishment: Comparative Studies in Detention, Incarceration, and Solitary Confinement*, Keramet Reiter and Alex Koenig, eds. (New York: Plagrave MacMillan, 2015), 177–96.

[7] Stanton and Walsh, "Was It Suicide?"

staffers renewed their requests, and every few hours, prison guards refused to comply. By the morning of September 7, Joseph Duran was dead in his cell.[8] The prison coroner labeled Joseph Duran's death a suicide, and closed the case. In 2013, the year that Duran died, a total of thirty prisoners would commit suicide in California prisons.[9] Between 2006 and 2010, an average of thirty-two prisoners per year committed suicide in California prisons.[10] This amounted to a rate of twenty-four suicides for every 100,000 prisoners in California, a shocking 50 percent above the average national rate of suicides in (or out of) prison.[11] Duran, then, was part of a substantial problem with suicides in California prisons.

Duran was also one among dozens of prisoners who had what amounted to substantial state assistance in killing themselves. Of the first fifteen suicides committed in 2012, the year before Duran died, three were not discovered for at least two hours, as evidenced by the onset of rigor mortis in the bodies prior to discovery. And thirteen of the first fifteen suicides in 2012 involved "inadequate assessment, treatment or intervention."[12] In March of 2013, about six months before Duran committed suicide, the expert appointed to monitor suicides and recommend policies to reduce the high suicide rates in California prisons, "quit out of frustration," publicly accusing prison officials of "being indifferent to suicide prevention."[13] When Duran died in September of 2013, his death was met with the same indifference that had exasperated the court appointed

---

[8] Ibid.

[9] Kent Imai, *Analysis of 2013 Inmate Death Reviews in the California Correctional Healthcare System*, California Correctional Healthcare Services, Oct. 27, 2014, 6, http://www.cphcs. ca.gov/docs/resources/OTRES_DeathReviewAnalysisYear2013_20141027.pdf.

[10] Sal Rodriguez, "California Prison Conditions Driving Prisoners to Suicide," *Solitary Watch*, Mar. 15, 2013, http://solitarywatch.com/2013/03/15/california-prison-conditions-driving-prisoners-to-suicide/.

[11] Abby Ohlheiser, "Expert Tasked with Solving California's Prison Suicide Problem Quits out of Frustration," *Slate*, Mar. 15, 2013, http://www.slate.com/blogs/the_slatest/2013/03/15/california_prison_suicides_federal_expert_quits_in_frustration_says_state.html; Centers for Disease Control and Prevention, *Fatal Injury Reports 1999-2015*, https://www.cdc.gov/injury/wisqars/fatal_injury_reports.html.

[12] "CDCR's Response to Dr. Raymond Patterson," *CDCR Today*, Mar. 14, 2013, http://cdcrtoday.blogspot.com/2013/03/cdcrs-response-to-dr-raymond-patterson.html.

[13] Ohlheiser, "Expert Tasked."

monitor. No one—not the courts, not Duran's family, not the media—was notified of his death.

Instead, four months later, in January of 2014, two investigative reporters with the daily newspaper based in California's capital city, the *Sacramento Bee*, uncovered the disturbing details of Duran's death. Sam Stanton and Denny Walsh explained when they first reported the story that it was based on "confidential documents obtained by the *Sacramento Bee*."[14] The mysterious "confidential" documents surprised everyone, including the lawyers litigating unconstitutional healthcare in California prisons and Joseph Duran's parents, Steve and Elaine Duran. The Durans first learned that Joseph had died when a *Sacramento Bee* reporter called them to ask for details about their son's life. He had been cremated almost four months earlier.

Four months might seem like a long time to be out of touch with a son, but as will be discussed in Chapter Five, phone calls from prison can be extremely expensive for families. Moreover, letters can take weeks to make it through prison censorship procedures and out of, or into, prison. Duran's parents explained that they had lost touch with him during his severe bouts with addiction and mental illness. They had thought he was probably safer housed in a Los Angeles jail, where they had last seen him, than roaming the streets.

Michael Bien, a lead lawyer litigating the lack of mental healthcare for prisoners in California since 1991, also learned of the details of Duran's death from *Sacramento Bee* reporters. When a reporter called him and asked him to assess the death reports, Bien said that, in his decades of litigating prison healthcare, he had "never seen anything like what happened to this man." He elaborated, questioning the "suicide" label, too: "Whether you call it suicide, neglect, accident, or deliberate indifference, to stand outside a cell and watch someone die, I've never heard of it."[15] As soon as he saw the documents the *Sacramento Bee* had obtained, Bien demanded a legal conference in the *Plata* case, insisting

---

[14] Stanton and Walsh, "Was it Suicide?"
[15] Ibid.

on an urgent meeting with the judge overseeing mental health issues in the litigation.[16]

Bien was especially frustrated that prison officials had not provided the documents describing Duran's death during a twenty-eight-day hearing that took place just weeks after Duran died. The hearing had focused on a rash of fact patterns that resembled Duran's experiences: unconstitutionally use of excessive use of force against prisoners with mental illnesses. In fact, one of the key issues during these hearings was the use of lachrymatory agents (pepper spray) in California prisons. The hearings involved videos of at least six different prisoners, naked and screaming for help, as prison officials doused them repeatedly with pepper spray.

Prison officials argued that pepper spray was merely an "irritant." A prison psychiatrist said that mentally ill prisoners "have a higher than average threshold for pain or noxious stimuli."[17] Local doctors responded in outrage, debunking this assertion in the *Los Angeles Times*.[18] And lawyers like Bien argued that pepper spray was overused and underregulated. That was before anyone even knew about Joseph Duran and how he had died.

Following the January 2014 story in the *Sacramento Bee*, California prison officials faced a new flurry of outraged attention. Judge Karlton, who had overseen the twenty-eight-day hearing on pepper spray and other uses of force against mentally ill prisoners in the fall of 2013, right after Duran had died, reopened his investigation into those issues. When a lawyer from the California Attorney General's office attempted to defend state prison officials, arguing that they had taken Duran's death

---

[16] Technically, much of the litigation in Duran's case revolved around claims in the *Coleman* litigation, a case specifically challenging inadequate provision of mental healthcare in California prisons. Federal judges later joined the *Coleman* case with the *Plata* case. Because of this, I simply refer to the *Plata* case throughout this section.

[17] Paige St. John, "California to Limit Pepper Spray Use On Mentally Ill Inmates," *Los Angeles Times*, Oct. 23, 2013, http://articles.latimes.com/2013/oct/23/local/la-me-ff-prisons-20131024.

[18] Thomas Blair, "Letters: Mentally ill, in prison," *Los Angeles Times*, Oct. 27, 2013, http://articles.latimes.com/2013/oct/27/opinion/la-le-1027-sunday-mental-illness-prison-20131027.

"extremely seriously from the beginning," Judge Karlton told the state's lawyer to use more "caution" in accepting prison officials' explanations.[19]

Joseph Duran's parents brought a lawsuit alleging wrongful death and seeking $6.75 million in damages. They argued that prison officials had attempted to hide their son's death from them, failing to notify them, and cremating his remains within a few days of his death. Prison officials ultimately settled the case for $750,000—reportedly "one of the largest [settlements] in the last decade in the Sacramento region resulting from conduct by prison officials."[20]

Meanwhile, prison officials still worked to mitigate the damage from the *Sacramento Bee's* exposé of the Duran case. They tried to figure out how in the world Sam Stanton and Denny Walsh had found out about Joseph Duran's death. They investigated people within the prison system who would have known about Duran's death, and they identified Eric Reininga, a psychologist, as a prime candidate. They followed his Facebook page and his wife's Facebook page and reviewed his private phone records, trying to build a case against him.

Dr. Reininga's job had been to review cases in which mentally ill prisoners had died and to write up reports assessing the circumstances of the prisoners' deaths. The reports had been mandated as part of the *Plata* litigation, and they were supposed to go directly to the panel of federal judges overseeing the healthcare reforms in California prisons. But Reininga said supervisors edited each of the reports he wrote to be more favorable to Department of Corrections interests. He described prison officials as "in a state of siege with the [*Plata*] court," resisting requirements to provide information, and resisting reforms.

When prison officials edited his report about Duran, though, Reininga lost patience. He could not stand knowing that Duran's parents would never know what had happened to their son, and he could not live with

---

[19] Paige St. John, "Judge Opens Inquiry into California Prison Death," *Los Angeles Times*, Jan. 30, 2014, http://articles.latimes.com/2014/jan/30/local/la-me-ff-judge-opens-inquiry-into-prison-death-20140130.

[20] Sam Stanton and Denny Walsh, "$750,000 Settlement Reached in Death of Inmate Pepper Sprayed in the Face," *Sacramento Bee*, Aug. 22, 2016, http://www.sacbee.com/news/local/crime/article97246522.html#storylink=cpy.

being a part of the "code of silence" covering up abuses. So he sent his report to the *Sacramento Bee*. In January of 2015, one year after Reininga sent his report to the *Bee*, prison officials confronted him with all the investigative work they had done on him. And they fired him. According to Reininga, in a deeply ironic outcome, he was the only prison official to face discipline after Duran's death.[21] Nothing happened, for instance, to Officer Chavez, who pepper sprayed Duran and left him in his cell, or to the unnamed officers who refused to remove Duran from his cell when doctors expressed concern about his well-being.

Though he was sent to Mule Creek for treatment, Duran had antagonized prison officials while there. But his treatment was part of a pattern of egregious mistreatment of mentally ill prisoners and avoidance of responsibility for this mistreatment. This was not just happening in California. In May of 2015, Human Rights Watch issued a report describing the "unnecessary, excessive, and even malicious force" used against mentally ill prisoners across the United States. Human Rights Watch recommended that public officials, like prison wardens, treat prisoners more humanely and that elected officials, like legislators, allocate resources to facilitate this.[22]

Duran's death epitomizes the challenges of simultaneously treating and punishing the mentally ill, including: How do institutional officials balance security concerns with medical concerns? Are any social institutions—whether prisons, hospitals, courts, or even investigative journalists—adequately equipped to protect the interests of these especially vulnerable prisoner-patients?

TRANSINSTITUTIONALIZATION: HOSPITAL OR PRISON?

The question of which institutions are best equipped to care for individuals like Joseph Duran has plagued politicians, courts, and administrators

---

[21] Sam Stanton and Denny Walsh, "Lawsuit Says 'Code of Silence' Hid California Inmate's Death," *Sacramento Bee*, Apr. 19, 2016, http://www.sacbee.com/news/local/crime/article72982367.html.

[22] Jamie Fellner, *Callous and Cruel: Use of Force against Inmates with Mental Disabilities in U.S. Prisons and Jails* (New York: Human Rights Watch, 2015), https://www.hrw.org/report/2015/05/12/callous-and-cruel/use-force-against-inmates-mental-disabilities-us-jails-and.

for decades. And the question remains pressing—given the prevalence of mental illness in the U.S. population in general and in prisons in particular. Roughly 18 percent of the U.S. population (or one in five adults) experiences mental illness each year, but only 4 percent of the U.S. population (one in twenty-five adults) has a "serious mental illness," defined as illness that results "in serious functional impairment, which substantially interferes with or limits one or more major life activities." For people suffering with mental illness in the general population, treatment rates are variable. Between 40 percent of those who have some mental health condition receive treatment in any given year, and 63 percent of those who have a serious mental illness receive treatment.[23]

By contrast, analysts at the Bureau of Justice Statistics—the national agency that gathers and assesses data about crime and punishment in the United States—estimate rates of some kind of mental illness among incarcerated people at 50 percent or higher, more than double the rate of mental illness outside of prison.[24] And as many as one quarter of prisoners have a serious mental illness, six times the rate of serious mental illness outside of prison.[25] While people with mental illness are overrepresented in prison, they also tend to be undertreated there; according to the Bureau of Justice Statistics, of those with known mental health problems, only one-third of state prisoners, one quarter of federal prisoners, and less than one-fifth of jail detainees receive treatment for those problems.[26] In California, one of the biggest state prison systems, more than 30,000 (one *quarter*) of the state's 120,000 prisoners have known, serious mental health needs. As Duran's case and the associated litigation revealed, California prison officials, like prison officials across the

---

[23] "Mental Health By the Numbers," National Alliance on Mental Illness, http://www .nami.org/Learn-More/Mental-Health-By-the-Numbers, "Serious Mental Illness Among U.S. Adults," National Institute of Mental Health, 2014, http://www.nimh.nih. gov/health/statistics/prevalence/serious-mental-illness-smi-among-us-adults.shtml.

[24] D.J. James and L.E. Glaze, *Mental Health Problems of Prison and Jail Inmates* (NCJ 213600) (Washington, DC: U.S. Department of Justice, Office of Justice Programs, Bureau of Justice Statistics, 2006), http://www.bjs.gov/content/pub/pdf/mhppji.pdf.

[25] *States That Provide Mental Health Alternatives to Solitary Confinement* (New York, Correctional Association of New York, 2008), http://www.correctionalassociation.org/ wp-content/uploads/2012/05/Out_of_State_Models.pdf.

[26] James and Glaze, *Mental Health Problems*.

United States, have significant challenges addressing prisoners' mental health needs.

Why this persistent overrepresentation and undertreatment of the mentally ill in prison? Pop psychology offers plenty of easy answers: prison is tough; people with bad coping skills end up in prison; people in prison feel removed from their families and stabilizing networks, or they do not get adequate care. But the real answer is more complicated. A broader perspective on institutions—not just prisons, but hospitals, too—is required.[27] In the United States in the twenty-first century, institutional actors (police, judges, prison officials) tend to treat lawbreakers as criminals first and mentally ill second. This prioritization of criminality over illness, in turn, means more prison beds are available than hospital beds.[28] This institutional perspective reveals that the mentally ill end up in prison because there is just nowhere else for them to go.

The current shortage of institutions to treat, rather than punish, the mentally ill dates to the middle of the twentieth century, around the time prisoners were beginning to argue that they had civil rights. So were psychiatric patients. In 1975, the U.S. Supreme Court heard *O'Connor v. Donaldson*, the first high court case assessing the rights of mental health patients civilly (as opposed to criminally) confined to hospitals against their will. *O'Connor* came just ten years after the prisoner civil rights cases *Robinson v. California* and *Cooper v. Pate*, discussed in Chapter One, which provided prisoners with legal mechanisms to challenge the conditions of their confinement. In the *O'Connor* case, Kenneth Donaldson, a civilly committed mental health patient, sought to assert rights similar to those prisoners had asserted in *Robinson* and *Cooper*.

In 1956, Kenneth Donaldson, then in his forties, went to visit his elderly parents in Florida. Donaldson's father became concerned that his son was suffering from delusions and had him civilly committed at the

---

[27] For two excellent academic works examining institutions as units of analysis, see Michel Foucault, *Discipline and Punish: The Birth of the Prison*, Alan Sheridan, Trans. (New York, Random House, 1995, orig. pub. 1977); Ervin Goffman, *Asylums: Essays on the Social Situation of Mental Patients and Other Inmates* (New York: Anchor Books, 1961).

[28] Thomas R. Blair, "The Trans-Allegheny Lunatic Asylum, Then and Now," *American Journal of Psychiatry* 171, no. 11 (Nov. 2014): 1160–61.

Florida State Hospital in Chattahoochee, following a hearing in front of a county judge. Donaldson repeatedly asserted that he was not mentally ill, and he refused treatment. He had no history of dangerousness, and accrued no record of dangerousness while confined. Yet his demands for release were denied—for fifteen years.

In 1971, Donaldson brought a Section 1983 lawsuit, the same kind of lawsuit Thomas Cooper brought to assert unequal or inconsistent treatment as a Muslim prisoner. The Florida court that first heard the case ordered Donaldson's release and assessed damages against O'Connor, the superintendent of the mental hospital where Donaldson had spent so much of his life. The Supreme Court agreed with the Florida decision that Donaldson's constitutional rights had been violated: "a State cannot constitutionally confine, without more [reason or evidence], a non-dangerous individual who is capable of surviving safely in freedom by himself or with the help of willing and responsible family members or friends."[29] The standard of "danger to self or others" would, to the present, come to dictate whether or not someone labeled as mentally ill could be forced into either treatment or confinement. But as with prisoners' rights litigation a decade earlier, these new rights for mental health patients also presented new problems for institutions of social control.

Cases like Donaldson's both highlighted the injustices that some patients experienced in U.S. mental hospitals and inspired horror among everyday citizens, who imagined being involuntarily confined for no good reason, with no recourse, among physically dangerous or floridly psychotic patients. Moreover, concerns abounded about whether psychiatric hospitals oppressed vulnerable groups of people. Historians have documented how mental hospitals were used to control all manner of socially challenging groups, from insufficiently submissive housewives in the 1950s to African American civil rights activists in the 1960s and 1970s.[30] In these contexts, civil rights for mental health patients made sense. But

---

[29] O'Connor v. Donaldson, 422 U.S. 563 (1975).

[30] See, e.g., Jonathan Metzl, *The Protest Psychosis: How Schizophrenia Became a Black Disease* (Boston: Beacon Press, 2011); Emily Thuma, "Against the 'Prison/Psychiatric State': Anti-Violence Feminisms and the Politics of Confinement in the 1970s," *Feminist Formations* 26, no. 2 (Summer 2014): 26–51.

as more of these cases were uncovered and litigated, they chipped away at the legitimacy of mental health institutions.

The media contributed to this delegitimization process, too. A series of exposés in widely read national news sources like *Life* magazine and *Reader's Digest* uncovered overcrowding, abuse, and neglect in psychiatric facilities across the United States.[31] One of the most upsetting exposés came out in 1972. Geraldo Rivera, a young TV reporter who would later become an acclaimed talk show host, visited the Willowbrook State School on Staten Island, in New York. Willowbrook was an institution for mentally ill and developmentally delayed children. There, Rivera not only found overcrowding and abuse, but he also discovered that residents had been systematically exposed to one of the viruses that causes hepatitis.[32] The exposure happened through deliberate injections and through feeding children contaminated feces, all part of an experiment being run by Doctor Saul Krugman at the New York University School of Medicine. Krugman eventually developed a hepatitis vaccine based on these controversial experiments.[33]

Within a few years of Rivera's exposé, Willowbrook was empty, its doors forever closed. Willowbrook, though, was only one of dozens of psychiatric hospitals to close down over the 1960s and 1970s during a process of mass *deinstitutionalization*.

This deinstitutionalization process started in California and New York as early as the 1950s. Public health professionals advocated for

---

[31] One of these "exposés" was the bestselling novel by Ken Kesey, *One Flew Over the Cuckoo's Nest* (Viking Press, 1962), which described and critiqued life in an Oregon psychiatric hospital. The book was made into a Broadway play in 1963 and an Academy Award-winning film in 1975.

[32] *See* Wesley Sheffield, "Still Pursuing the Promise of Reform Fifty Years Later," Young Minds Advocacy, Oct. 31, 2013, https://www.youngmindsadvocacy.org/the-community-mental-health-act-of-1963/; "Remembering an Infamous New York Institution," *NPR, Southern California Public Radio*, Mar. 7, 2008, http://www.npr.org/templates/story/story.php?storyId=87975196; *Geraldo: Willowbrook State School*, http://www.geraldo.com/folio/willowbrook (includes links to excerpts from the original documentary).

[33] For a description of the experiments, and a review of the ethical debates surrounding them, see National Institutes of Health, "Module 5, Research Ethics: The Power and Peril of Human Experimentation," 5.4, https://science.education.nih.gov/supplements/nih9/bioethics/guide/pdf/master_5-4.pdf.

the importance of local and community mental health services as alternatives to state hospitalizations, and secured state legislation to support such initiatives.[34] In the 1960s, new federal lawmaking brought national attention and legitimacy to the deinstitutionalization movement. Specifically, President Kennedy signed the Community Mental Health Act (CMHA) into law in October of 1963, just a few weeks before he was assassinated. The CMHA provided $3 billion in federal funds to establish community mental health centers. At the time, there were roughly 500,000 people confined in psychiatric institutions across the United States. Kennedy's CMHA responded to the growing body of stories criticizing the conditions these half-a-million people were experiencing and provided a remedy: replace locked psychiatric facilities with community centers designed to provide outpatient and short-term inpatient care to mentally ill people, who would remain in their communities.[35]

In one sense, CMHA worked incredibly well. In fewer than two decades, America's psychiatric hospitals would be largely abandoned, a few even becoming sites of ghost tours and haunted houses.[36] By 1980, public psychiatric hospitals had only one-quarter as many inpatients as they had had in the 1960s. By 2000, public psychiatric hospitals had just one-tenth as many inpatients as they had had in the 1960s. The institutionalized population hovered around 50,000.[37]

Although state mental hospitals lost both legitimacy and funding over the latter half of the twentieth century, the community treatment centers President Kennedy envisioned never received adequate funding to support the growing population of deinstitutionalized people with mental illness across the United States.[38] Instead, people kicked out of shuttered institutions ended up homeless on the streets, or, worse, arrested and

---

[34] Gerald N. Grob, "The Forging of Mental Health Policy in America: World War II to New Frontier," *Journal of the History of Medicine and Allied Sciences* 42 (1987): 410–46, 430.

[35] See Sheffield, "Still Pursuing the Promise."

[36] Blair, "The Trans-Allegheny Lunatic Asylum." See also Gerald Grob, *The Mad Among Us* (New York: Free Press, 2010).

[37] Grob, *The Mad Among Us.*

[38] Ibid.

reinstitutionalized in jails and prisons.[39] By the 1990s, scholars had a new name for this process: *transinstitutionalization.*

Psychiatrist James Gilligan and legal scholar Bernard Harcourt have both examined the transinstitutionalization of the mentally ill from locked psychiatric institutions into prisons and jails. Gilligan has noted the growth of "prison psychiatry" as a specialized medical practice in the United States, and dubbed prisons as "the last mental hospitals."[40] Indeed, the deinstitutionalization of psychiatric hospitals, facilitated in particular by the passage of Kennedy's CMHA in 1963, coincided with increasing rates of incarceration, beginning in the 1970s.

Harcourt describes deinstitutionalization and mass incarceration as correlated, but traces how mentally ill prisoners are just one of many subpopulations contributing to the growth of imprisonment in the United States.[41] In other words, even though there were a half million people in psychiatric institutions in the 1960s, not all of those people went directly to prisons in the 1970s and 1980s. And deinstitutionalization of the mentally ill in the 1960s cannot alone explain the steep increase in incarceration in the 1970s. Nonetheless, deinstitutionalization was one critical component of mass incarceration. Studies estimate that, as rates of incarceration expanded between 1980 and 2000, the deinstitutionalization of mentally ill people accounted for 4 to 7 percent of incarceration growth.[42]

Even if there is limited empirical evidence of a direct conversion of deinstitutionalized mentally ill patients into institutionalized mentally ill criminals, jails and prisons have undoubtedly become the default institutional placement for people with mental illness. By the early 2000s, America's largest jails—the municipal jails for Chicago, Los Angeles,

---

[39] Pete Earley, *Crazy: A Father's Search Through America's Mental Health Madness* (New York: Penguin Group, 2006).

[40] James Gilligan, "The Last Mental Hospital," *Psychiatric Quarterly* 72, no. 1 (2001): 45–61.

[41] Bernard E. Harcourt, "Reducing Mass Incarceration: Lessons from the Deinstitutionalization of Mental Hospitals in the 1960s," *Ohio State Journal of Criminal Law* 9 (2011): 53–88.

[42] Steven Raphael and Michael A. Stoll, "Assessing the Contribution of the Deinstitutionalization of the Mentally Ill to Growth in the U.S. Incarceration Rate," *Journal of Legal Studies* 42, no. 1 (January 2013): 187–222.

and New York—doubled as the country's three largest psychiatric hospitals.[43] Scholars estimate that today, in the United States, three times more people with serious mental illnesses are confined in jails and prisons than are confined in psychiatric hospitals.[44]

Joseph Duran's history of serious mental illness, suicide attempts, and low-level criminal arrests, resulting in perpetual cycling in and out of jail and prison, is representative of the experiences of many mentally ill Americans today. Fifty years ago, Duran would have been at least as likely to be housed in a psychiatric facility as in a jail or prison. Of course, experiences like Kenneth Donaldson's involuntary and indefinite commitment in a Florida psychiatric hospital, along with Geraldo Rivera's horrifying exposé of the Willowbrook State School, raise the question of whether Duran would have been treated any more humanely in a psychiatric hospital than in the mental health crisis unit at Mule Creek State Prison.

Today, thanks to ongoing reforms of the rules governing hospital-based mental health care—for the limited mental health in-patient beds that do exist—Duran likely would have received better care in a twenty-first century psychiatric hospital than he received at the Mule Creek prison. In California psychiatric hospitals, for instance, restraint and seclusion are both subject to strict regulations: doctors must order either restriction; healthcare providers must document face-to-face evaluations every hour; the restraint or seclusion order must be renewed every one to four hours, depending on the age of the patient; and such orders may be maintained for no more than twenty-four hours at a time.[45] In a psychiatric hospital, then, a healthcare provider would have been evaluating Duran's status every hour during his seclusion, rather than being turned away every few hours, while prison officials watched Duran die.

[43] Earley, *Crazy*; E. Fuller Torrey, *Care of the Seriously Mentally Ill: A Rating of State Programs* (Washington, DC: Public Citizen Health Research Group, 1990).

[44] E. F. Torrey, A. D. Kennard, D. Eslinger, R. Lamb, and J. Pavle, *More Mentally Ill Persons Are in Jails and Prisons Than Hospitals: A Survey of the States*, Treatment Advocacy Center & National Sheriff's Association, 2010, http://www.treatmentadvocacycenter.org/storage/documents/final_jails_v_hospitals_study.pdf.

[45] *Compilation of Select Laws & Regulations Regarding Behavioral Restraint & Seclusion*, Pub. 5457.01, Oakland: Disability Rights California, 2014, http://www.disabilityrightsca.org/pubs/545701.pdf.

Moreover, since 1977, disability rights advocates, usually in the form of state-level "protection and advocacy" organizations (P&As), have had federal authority to monitor care providers and to assist with legal and advocacy needs, in order to ensure the adequate provision of care to people with disabilities.[46] Since 1986, P&A authority has included oversight on behalf of people with mental illnesses, per congressional authorization.[47] Increasingly, these P&As are seeking to exercise this authority to monitor and enforce regulations governing the treatment of people with disabilities in prisons, as well as in hospitals and other residential facilities. In states like Washington and Nevada, the P&As have used their monitoring authority to visit prisoners with mental illnesses in solitary confinement, in particular, and have advocated for better treatment of these prisoners, more in line with the standards governing treatment in hospital and other residential settings.[48] In practice, however, the standards governing treatment of people with mental illness in hospital settings are significantly more protective (and subject to more and more rigorous oversight) than the standards governing people with mental illness in prison settings.

The debates about what rights the mentally ill have, and how these rights should be balanced with institutional obligations to maintain safety and security for inpatients and surrounding communities, echo the debates that were raised in both Larry Hope's hitching post litigation and Marciano Plata's healthcare litigation, and by the hunger striking prisoners in the Pelican Bay solitary confinement units, too. In hospitals as in prisons, reconciling individual rights (whether those of Kenneth

[46] For a description of these P&As, see "Administration on Intellectual and Developmental Disabilities (AIDD): State Protection and Advocacy System," Washington, DC: U.S. Department of Health and Human Services, Administration for Community Living, https://acl.gov/programs/aidd/Programs/PA/index.aspx.

[47] For an overview of the history of P&As, see "History," The Protection and Advocacy System for South Carolina, http://www.pandasc.org/about/history/.

[48] See Anna Guy, *Locked Up and Locked Down: Segregation of Inmates with Mental Illness* (Seattle, AVID (Amplifying Voices of Inmates with Disabilities) and Disability Rights Washington, 2016), http://avidprisonproject.org/; Katie Rose Quandt, with Helen Zaikina-Montgomery, *Unlocking Solitary Confinement: Ending Extreme Isolation in Nevada State Prisons* (The ACLU of Nevada, Solitary Watch, and Nevada Disability Advocacy & Law Center, Feb. 2017), https://www.aclunv.org/sites/default/files/aclunv_unlocking_solitary_confinement_report.pdf.

Donaldson or of Joseph Duran) with institutional imperatives creates perpetual social and governmental challenges. Are civil and human rights ever compatible with locked institutions, whether hospitals or prisons?

SOLITARY CONFINEMENT AND MENTAL HEALTH

Joseph Duran's story is not just representative of the well-known correlation between mental illness and incarceration; it is also representative of a lesser-known and often unnoticed correlation between mental illness, suicide, and incarceration specifically in solitary confinement. An estimated 33 to 50 percent of all prisoners in solitary confinement have a serious mental illness; that is as much as double the estimated 25 percent of prisoners with serious mental illnesses in the general prison population.[49] Solitary confinement is, in fact, the default placement for mentally ill prisoners in many prison systems—whether because symptoms of mental illness are categorized and treated as defiant rule-breaking, or because there is simply no other safe place to house these challenging prisoners.[50]

Not only are the seriously mentally ill overrepresented in solitary confinement, but they are especially likely to get worse while isolated. Isolation can cause new mental health problems and exacerbate existing ones.[51] Unsurprisingly, then, a disproportionate number of prison suicides take place in solitary confinement. At any given time, between 2 and 8 percent of a state's prison population is in solitary confinement. But state-by-state, 50 percent, or more, of prison suicides take place in solitary confinement.[52] In 2005, a peak year for California prison suicides, 70 percent of the suicides in the state's prisons took place in solitary

[49] *States That Provide Mental Health Alternatives.*

[50] For a policy overview of this over-representation of the mentally ill, with a profile of a handful of state policies, see Guy, *Locked Up and Locked Down.*

[51] Stuart Grassian, "Psychiatric Effects of Solitary Confinement," *Washington University Journal of Law and Policy* 22 (2006): 325–383, 333.

[52] Daniel P. Mears, *Evaluating the Effectiveness of Supermax Prisons* (Washington, D.C.: U.S. Department of Justice, 2006); Terry Kupers, "What to Do with Survivors? Coping with the Long Term Effects of Isolate Confinement," *Criminal Justice and Behavior* 35, no. 8 (2008): 1005–16, at 1009.

confinement units.[53] Of the suicides plaguing the California prisons between 2006 and 2013, more than 40 percent—almost half—took place in solitary confinement cells, including mental health crisis units, like the one in which Joseph Duran was housed.[54] Similar disparities exist in other states that have compared suicide rates outside of solitary confinement to suicide rates in solitary confinement. For instance, in New York City's Rikers Island jail, suicide is seven times more common in solitary confinement than in the general population. In Indiana state prisons, suicide is three times more common in solitary confinement than in the general prison population.[55]

Although the relationship between mass incarceration and mental illness has been documented by psychiatrists, lawyers, economists, and statisticians, scholars are just beginning to examine this even more disturbing phenomenon of the overrepresentation of the mentally ill in solitary confinement in prisons across the United States. Expansions in the use of solitary confinement, it turns out, overlap with the already parallel histories of deinstitutionalization and mass incarceration. As prison populations expanded—and as the mentally ill were de- and transinstitutionalized—the use of isolation across the United States also expanded.

First, prison officials responded to prisoner organizing for civil rights (as described in Chapter One), as well as to unrest, violence, and uprisings in prison, by locking prisoners "down" into their cells for weeks, and then months, at a time.[56] Then, states began to medicalize these experiments with long-term segregation and confinement, dubbing some units "behavioral management units" and others "treatment centers" for the dangerous and violent. In reality, the behavior management often consisted

[53] Don Thompson, "Record California Inmate Suicides Are Double National Rate," *Free Republic*, Jan. 2, 2006, http://www.freerepublic.com/focus/f-news/1550815/ posts.

[54] Rodriguez, "California Prison Conditions."

[55] Fatos Kaba, Andrea Lewis, Sarah Glowa-Kollisch, James Hadler, David Lee, Howard Alper, Daniel Selling, et al., "Solitary Confinement and Risk of Self-Harm Among Jail Inmates," *American Journal of Public Health* 104, no. 3 (2014): 442–47; *Indiana Protection and Advocacy Services Commission v. Commissioner, Indiana Dept. of Correction*, Case No. 1:08-CV-01317 TWPMJD, (S.D. Ind. Dec. 31, 2012), at *16.

[56] See Keramet Reiter, *23/7: Pelican Bay Prison and the Rise of Long-Term Solitary Confinement* (New Haven, Yale University Press, 2016): 34–58.

of stripping prisoners of all rights, or forcibly medicating them.[57] Next, states began to build supermaxes, like the Pelican Bay Security Housing Unit that prisoners protested through hunger strikes in the 2010s (as described in Chapter One), to institutionalize these lockdown conditions. Arizona opened the first of these supermaxes, designed for long-term solitary confinement, in 1986, and California opened two of the biggest in 1988 and 1989.[58] As prison populations grew throughout the 1980s, states built dozens of new prisons to keep up with this population growth; in nearly every state, as well as in the federal prison system, prison officials also added at least one supermax.[59] Today, at least 80,000 prisoners in the United States are in some form of solitary confinement, whether shorter-term segregation (around thirty days), like Joseph Duran was in at Mule Creek State Prison, or longer-term supermaximum security confinement (months to years), like the hunger striking prisoners in the Pelican Bay Security Housing Unit.[60]

As the early history of lockdowns and supermaxes suggests, solitary confinement comes by many names and has many purposes, including: disciplinary segregation (for rule-breakers), administrative segregation (for threatening or dangerous prisoners, whether they broke a rule or not), mental health crisis segregation (for the acutely mentally ill), behavior management (for those in need of "retraining"), and protective custody (for those who are unsafe in general prison populations). Across every category of solitary confinement, there is one common theme: isolated prisoners tend to be the ones who are the toughest for prison staff to

[57] See ibid.; Thuma, "Against the 'Prison/Psychiatric State.'"

[58] Mona Lynch, *Sunbelt Justice: Arizona and the Transformation of American Punishment* (Stanford: Stanford University Press, 2010); Keramet Reiter, "Parole, Snitch or Die: California's Supermax Prisons and Prisoners, 1997–2007," *Punishment & Society* 14, no. 5 (2012): 530–63.

[59] Alexandra Naday, Joshua D. Freilich, and Jeff Mellow, "The Elusive Data on Supermax Confinement," *The Prison Journal* 88, no. 1 (Mar. 2008): 69–93; Chase Riveland, *Supermax Prisons: Overview and General Considerations* (Washington, D.C.: U.S. Department of Justice, National Institute of Corrections, 1999), http://www.nicic.org/pubs/1999/014937.pdf.

[60] J. J. Gibbons and N. D. Katzenbach, "Confronting Confinement: A Report of the Commission On Safety and Abuse in America's Prisons," *Washington University Journal of Law and Policy* 22 (2006): 385–562.

manage, whether because they are participating in protests, threatening staff, having trouble following rules, being vulnerable, or simply experiencing untreated mental illness.

Prisoners with mental illness especially tend to have a range of problems that might land them in any of the many forms of solitary confinement. Sometimes, as in Joseph Duran's case, mentally ill prisoners are assigned to solitary for "treatment." At other times, mentally ill prisoners have difficulty following prison rules and end up in solitary for nominally "punitive" reasons. Bradley Ballard's story is a good example of this.

Ballard was seemingly even more seriously mentally ill than Joseph Duran; in spite of the rarity of psychiatric hospitalization in the 2000s, Ballard had spent five weeks in a psychiatric hospital in 2014. Shortly after, he was arrested for assault and public lewdness and taken to Rikers Island, New York City's jail complex. At Rikers, Ballard continued his pattern of lewd behavior, gesturing at a female officer. Prison officials disciplined him by moving him into solitary confinement. In solitary confinement, he stopped up his toilet. This time, prison officials disciplined him by turning off the water line supplying his cell. Ballard's misbehavior only escalated with each punishment; once the water line was turned off, he tied a rubber band around his genitals and smeared himself in feces. Prison officials refused to let him out of his cell and stopped medicating him. He passed out, no one entered his cell to check on him, and he died of sepsis in May of 2014.[61]

Ballard and Duran illustrate big-picture data: mental illness has become a risk factor for assignment to solitary confinement, whether for treatment or punishment.[62] Worse, placement in solitary confinement is a risk factor for further mental deterioration—again as both Duran and Ballard experienced. Based only on the statistics about the high rates of suicide among those prisoners in solitary confinement, isolated prisoners seem more likely to lose hope and to find a way to take their own lives than non-isolated prisoners. Indeed, a robust body of literature has

[61] J. Pearson, "AP Exclusive: Inmate Died After 7 Days in NYC Cell', *The Big Story*, May 22, 2014, http://bigstory.ap.org/article/ap-exclusive-inmate-died-after-7-days- nyc-cell.

[62] For an elaboration on this and the discussion in this section generally, see Reiter and Blair, "Punishing Mental Illness," 177–96.

documented that solitary confinement can have a range of serious mental health consequences, even after a few days, and even for prisoners who were previously psychologically stable. These consequences include anxiety, depression, insomnia, hallucinations, and full-blown delirium. One psychiatrist dubbed the constellation of psychological effects associated with solitary confinement "SHU Syndrome," arguing that solitary confinement produces "major, clinically distinguishable" symptoms.[63] In a comprehensive review of the effects of solitary confinement, published in 1997, psychologists Craig Haney and Mona Lynch noted consensus in the research they reviewed that solitary confinement inflicts "psychological trauma."[64]

Some critics argue, however, that these studies of the mental health dangers of solitary confinement are based on small samples of prisoners, many of whom were interviewed or evaluated as part of litigation challenging the conditions of their confinement, rather than as part of systematic, or experimental studies.[65] One recent study, conducted in Colorado, sought to use a quasi-experimental design—with matched samples to approximate random assignment to "treatment" groups in solitary confinement and "control" groups in general prison populations—to assess the psychological impacts of solitary confinement.[66] Although the study concluded that solitary confinement was not as bad for mental health as previous studies had found, it was subsequently criticized for having a flawed experimental design, with reliance on prisoners' own self-reports about their moods, and selective reporting of results, including dropping one prisoner participant, who committed suicide while in solitary confinement, from

[63] Stuart Grassian, "Psychopathological effects of solitary confinement," *American Journal of Psychiatry* 140, no. 11 (1983): 1450–4.

[64] Craig Haney and Mona Lynch, "Regulating Prisons of the Future: a Psychological Analysis of Supermax and Solitary Confinement," *New York University Review of Law and Social Change* 23, no. 4 (1997): 477–570.

[65] See, for instance, the debate on the podcast *Shrink Rap*, posted here: ClinkShrink, "Leave Me Alone: Does SHU Syndrome Exist?" *Shrink Rap*, Jun. 11, 2008, http://psychiatrist-blog.blogspot.com/2008/06/leave-me-alone-does-shu-syndrome-exist.html.

[66] Maureen L. O'Keefe, Kelli J. Klebe, Alysha Stucker, Kristin Sturm, and William Leggett, *One Year Longitudinal Study of the Psychological Effects of Administrative Segregation*, Doc. No. 232973 (Washington: National Criminal Justice Research Service, National Institute of Justice, 2011), www.ncjrs.gov/pdffiles1/nij/grants/232973.pdf.

the analysis and findings reports.[67] While the Colorado study is one of the few pieces of research to suggest the effects of solitary confinement on mental health might be exaggerated, it also ironically provided yet another example of a prisoner in isolation committing suicide.

The findings in the Colorado study aside, courts reviewing the constitutionality of conditions in solitary confinement have recognized the potentially dangerous consequences of solitary for mentally ill prisoners. Advocates have argued that placing prisoners with mental illnesses in solitary confinement violates the Eighth Amendment prohibition against cruel and unusual punishment, as well as the Americans with Disabilities Act (ADA), a federal statute guaranteeing equal treatment to people with disabilities.[68] In most cases, courts have ordered prison officials to ensure that seriously mentally ill prisoners are not placed in long-term solitary confinement, and that seriously mentally ill prisoners in short-term solitary confinement have access to treatment, natural light, and more out-of-cell time than non-seriously-mentally-ill prisoners.[69]

Such protections, however, fail to account for prisoners who develop symptoms of mental illness only after they are placed in solitary confinement; for prisoners like Ballard, who disobey correctional staff because of mental illness but get labeled as "bad" instead of "mad"; or for prisoners like Duran, who are labeled mentally ill and are ostensibly receiving treatment, but deteriorate further anyway. In historical perspective, solitary confinement actually served as a "linchpin" of transinstitutionalization— a key mechanism for moving people with mental illness from asylums to prisons.[70] As people with mental illness were deinstitutionalized out of locked psychiatric facilities, placed in communities, and ultimately reinstitutionalized in prisons and jails, solitary confinement became a critical tool deployed by prison officials to manage this especially challenging subpopulation of prisoners.

[67] Stuart Grassian, "'Fatal Flaws' in the Colorado Solitary Confinement Study," *Solitary Watch*, Nov. 15, 2010, http://solitarywatch.com/ 2010/11/15/fatal-flaws-in-the-colorado -solitary-confinement-study/.

[68] Guy, *Locked Up and Locked Down*.

[69] See, e.g., *Madrid v. Gomez*, 889 F. Supp. 1146 (N.D. Cal. 1995); Reiter, *23/7*, 139.

[70] Reiter and Blair, "Punishing Mental Illness."

Not only are mentally ill prisoners more likely to end up in solitary confinement and more likely to deteriorate further once they are in solitary confinement, they also have trouble earning their way out of solitary confinement. Mentally ill prisoners in isolation often rack up additional disciplinary infractions, just as both Duran and Ballard did, making it increasingly difficult for them to "earn" their way out of solitary confinement through good behavior.[71] In fact, as prisoners deteriorate in solitary confinement, they often seem more and more like people who need to remain in solitary confinement, because they could not possibly function in a general prison population. Think of both Joseph Duran and Bradley Ballard. How could prisoners making faces and lewd gestures, pulling out tracheal tubes, and smearing their own feces around possibly survive in a general prison population? And how could prison staff, lacking training in handling and treating people with severe mental illness, be expected to manage these prisoners?

ETHICS OF CONFINEMENT: TO PUNISH OR TO PROTECT?

The confluence of mass incarceration, transinstitutionalization, and solitary confinement presents special challenges for healthcare providers, like the ones charged with treating both Joseph Duran and Bradley Ballard. In Duran's case, recall that a medical doctor ordered him removed from his cell after he was pepper sprayed, so that he could be decontaminated and his tracheal tube reinserted, and then medical staffers subsequently renewed the initial doctor's request. Why and how were the medical orders, requests, and recommendations ignored in Duran's case? The limited record obtained by the *Sacramento Bee* during their investigation into Duran's death provides few clues. But the question itself reveals a fundamental challenge of having the mentally ill incarcerated in a prison rather than in a hospital: prison guards' mandates to protect prisoners, themselves, and society perpetually conflict with medical providers' mandates

---

[71] See generally Lorna A. Rhodes, *Total Confinement: Madness and Reason in the Maximum Security Prison* (Berkeley: University of California Press, 2004); David Lovell, "Patterns of Disturbed Behavior in a Supermax Population," *Criminal Justice and Behavior* 35, no. 8 (2008): 985–1004.

to care for the ill. In prison settings, the guards' mandate all too often takes precedence over the care providers' mandate.

Providers of prison health services—whether nurses, therapists, or doctors—must grapple constantly with their institutional roles, deciding when and whether to insist on care, often at the risk of compromising protection.[72] In a study of the role of healthcare providers for prisoners being considered for placement in solitary confinement in the New York City jails, researchers found that healthcare providers frequently experienced a problem of *dual loyalty*. Prison officials asked clinicians to engage in healthcare assessments, such as whether or not a prisoner was mentally fit enough to be placed in solitary confinement, but then pressured clinicians into reaching conclusions that deferred to the "punishment process of the security apparatus," like clearing prisoners for placement in solitary confinement, whether or not placement was medically acceptable. Even where a patient was assessed to be psychologically resilient enough for placement in solitary confinement, clinicians worried that their role in legitimizing the placement compromised their relationships with their patients later. The study authors recommended that clinicians simply stop participating in these kinds of assessments.[73] But critics argued that, if clinicians stopped assessing prisoners prior to placement in solitary confinement, prisoners would lose a checkpoint that potentially protects them from solitary confinement. These critics suggested that, perhaps, if clinicians agreed that solitary confinement is dangerous for prisoners, they should evaluate prisoners for placement, but be more liberal in refusing to clear prisoners for such placements.[74]

---

[72] For an overview of these challenges, see Nancy Dubler, "Ethical Dilemmas In Prison And Jail Health Care," *Health Affairs Blog*, Mar. 10, 2014, http://healthaffairs.org/blog/2014/03/10/ethical-dilemmas-in-prison-and-jail-health-care/.

[73] Sarah Glowa-Kollisch, Jasmine Graves, Nathaniel Dickey, Ross MacDonald, Zachary Rosner, Anthony Waters, and Homer Venters, "Data-Driven Human Rights: Using Dual Loyalty Trainings to Promote the Care of Vulnerable Patients in Jail," *Health and Human Rights Journal* 17 (Mar. 12, 2016), https://www.hhrjournal.org/2015/03/data-driven-human-rights-using-dual-loyalty-trainings-to-promote-the-care-of-vulnerable-patients-in-jail/.

[74] Thomas R. Blair and Keramet A. Reiter, "Solitary Confinement and Mental Illness: Ethical Challenges for Clinicians; in response to Glowa-Kollisch et al.," *Health and Human Rights Journal*, http://www.hhrjournal.org/2015/07/02/letter-to-the-editor-and-author-response-solitary-confinement-and-mental-illness/.

A recent *New Yorker* feature story about clinicians working in an isolation unit for mentally ill prisoners, where guards frequently abused the prisoners, further reveals the challenges clinicians face in navigating the "punishment process of the security apparatus" while upholding basic standards of care. The feature profiled Harriet Krzykowski, a psychiatric technician charged with working with prisoners with behavioral problems in a Transitional Care Unit (TCU) in a prison in Miami, Florida. From her first day working at the prison, Krzykowski noticed problems in how the prisoners were treated—from not being fed adequately, to not being permitted out of their cells, to not being allowed to participate in mandated group activities. Krzykowski described how, after she reported some of these concerns to her supervisor, guards started leaving her alone with groups of prisoners—in treatment sessions, out on the prison yard, and in hallways filled with prisoners—as she was waiting for guards to open doors to allow her to pass through. She felt intimidated and was afraid for her own safety and her job security—such that when she heard about even worse abuses, she decided to stay quiet.

About two years after she started working at the Miami TCU, Krzykowski came to work on a Sunday morning and learned that a prisoner, about whom she had been worried the night before, because he had smeared himself in his own feces (like Ballard had on Rikers Island), had died overnight. When she inquired about his death, Krzykowski learned that guards had locked Darren Rainey in a shower stall, and then hosed him down with 180-degree water, until 90 percent of his skin peeled off, and he collapsed. Krzykowski was horrified. But she was too scared for her safety in the prison, and too scared to jeopardize the meager income of the job with which she supported her family, to seriously consider reporting the incident to authorities outside of the prison. Two years later, however, she supported and encouraged a prisoner, who had witnessed Rainey's death, to write about what he had seen, because she thought it would be therapeutically helpful for him in processing the traumatic memory. That prisoner eventually got in contact with a reporter, who investigated and wrote about the story of Rainey's death. No one commented at the time, but the fact that another prisoner came forward with the details of Rainey's death, instead of any one of the many mental health or clinical professionals working on the unit explicitly as "treatment" staff, was surprising.[75]

Were the many health care professionals working on the Miami TCU where Darren Rainey died all scared? Or were they all comfortable with compromising medical ethics and obligations in favor of security concerns and justifications? In such an abusive environment, refusing to evaluate prisoners for placement in solitary confinement or eligibility for other punishments, as the New York City jail researchers recommended (in order to avoid dual loyalties), would have little effect. Guards would simply inflict punishments on their own terms. Likewise, evaluating prisoners for placement in solitary confinement or eligibility for other punishments, but refusing to "clear" them, as the critics of the New York City jail researchers recommended, would be just as futile in an environment where that decision would spawn near-certain retaliation against the clinician.

The patterns of abuse described here in Florida (Darren Rainey), New York (Bradley Ballard), and California (Joseph Duran) have been repeated across the United States, often specifically involving mentally ill prisoners, who are in solitary confinement twenty-three or more hours of most days, and clinicians, who cannot or will not provide adequate care or relief. In states that have tried to develop systematic solutions to these kinds of abuses, the answer has often been to shift treatment contexts back from prisons to hospitals.

For instance, Bridgewater State Hospital in Massachusetts has long been a hybrid institution—housing the "criminally insane," sometimes in

---

[75] Eyal Press, "Madness," *New Yorker*, May 2, 2016, http://www.newyorker.com/magazine/2016/05/02/the-torturing-of-mentally-ill-prisoners. In 2017, after a lengthy investigation, Florida officials published a report in which they concluded there was no wrongdoing in the death of Darren Rainey. Kathleen Hoague and Johnette Hardiman, "In Custody Death Investigation Close-Out Memo, DAREN RAINEY," http://www.miamisao.com/pdfs/DarrenRaineyincustodydeathcloseoutmemo.pdf. Local media, however, sharply criticized the findings of the report and pointed to strong evidence of other, pervasive abuses in local prison facilities. See, e.g., Julie K. Brown, "Inmate accuser in Darren Rainey prison shower death feared a whitewash," *Miami Herald*, Mar. 23, 2017, http://www.miamiherald.com/news/special-reports/florida-prisons/article140444343.html; Julie K. Brown, "Graphic photos stir doubts about Darren Rainey's 'accidental' prison death," *Miami Herald*, May 6, 2017, http://www.miamiherald.com/news/local/community/miami-dade/article149026764.html.

more hospital-like settings and other times in more prison-like settings. In each iteration, however, Bridgewater has been plagued by allegations of abuse from its inhabitants. It began as an almshouse for the poor in the 1850s, but was eventually converted into a hospital for the criminally insane, remaining a hybrid institution with both noncriminal and criminal patients. In the 1960s, Bridgewater faced allegations of both abuse and barbarous treatment (as at Willowbrook, which Geraldo Rivera exposed) and holding patients and prisoners illegally (as at the Florida State Hospital in Chattahoochee, where Kenneth Donaldson was held for decades). In 1967, Frederick Wiseman made the documentary *Titicut Follies*, which exposed abuses from force-feeding, to overtranquilizing, to denial of clothing at Bridgewater.

Just twenty years later, in 1987, eight patients in one year died in the prison hospital, and the *New York Times* investigated, uncovering persistent, rampant abuses.[76] Most recently, the *Boston Globe* uncovered abuses of Bridgewater prisoners in the early 2000s: a twenty-three-year-old died when he was wrestled into restraints in 2009; a forty-three-year-old died after multiple suicide attempts while on alleged high-surveillance suicide watch in 2016; and records revealed that Bridgewater patients were placed in isolation at one hundred times the rate of patients in other state hospitals.[77] Bridgewater is now undergoing a transition back to a more hospital-like, rather than prison-like environment. In September of 2016, the Massachusetts governor ordered a series of reforms to the Bridgewater facility: removing criminally convicted prisoners from its population to facilitate refocusing on caring for the mentally ill; limiting contact

[76] "Deaths at a Prison Hospital Lead to Inquiries," *New York Times*, Jul. 19, 1987, http://www.nytimes.com/1987/07/19/us/deaths-at-a-prison-hospital-lead-to-inquiries.html.

[77] Michael Rezendes, "A Death in Restraints after 'standard procedure,'" *Boston Globe*, Feb. 16, 2014, http://www.bostonglobe.com/metro/2014/02/16/homicide-bridgewater-state-hospital-raises-profound-questions-about-care-for-mentally-ill/TqgMJdNZ8SPjLcFQ6hRkTN/story.html; *Death Investigation at Bridgewater State Hospital: Findings and Recommendations* (Boston, Disability Rights Center, Jun. 27 2016), http://www.dlc-ma.org/bsh/Public%20Report%20-%20Another%20Senseless%20Death%20at%20Bridgewater%20Final.pdf; Michael Rezendes, "Bridgewater Restraints Use Rose, Even After Patient's Death," *Boston Globe*, Apr. 6, 2014, http://www.bostonglobe.com/metro/2014/04/05/bridgewater-restraints-use-rose-even-after-patient-death/iVt77HVAplzKD5Eh3vaF4M/story.html.

between prisoner-patients and guards while expanding contact between prisoner-patients and clinicians; and generally transitioning toward a psychiatric hospital model.[78]

These changes implicitly concede that prison-like facilities face myriad difficulties in providing care to people with mental illness, whether or not the institutionalized person has also been convicted of crimes. But the changes also signal a reversion to an old model of care: institutionalizing people with serious mental illness and re-funding state psychiatric hospitals. Is the transinstitutionalization of the mentally ill from psychiatric facilities into prisons, and especially into solitary confinement, reversing? If so, will this lead to better conditions for prisoners or patients? Put another way, would more and better care have spared the lives of Joseph Duran, Bradley Ballard, and Darren Rainey?

In state psychiatric facilities, like New York's Willowbrook and Massachusetts's Bridgewater, the mentally ill have been abused, just as they have been abused in state prisons, especially in solitary confinement, in places like California's Mule Creek and Florida's Transitional Care Unit. In each of these cases, the abuses have been hidden behind locked institutional doors—exposed only by brave whistleblowers or persistent investigative journalists. Perhaps the community mental health centers reformers envisioned and Kennedy sought to establish in the 1960s deserve to be reconsidered as viable alternatives—if only because they would be, by definition, more visible than the hidden institutions where so many abuses have taken place over the last half-century.

---

[78] David Scharfenberg, "Baker Calls for Change in Treating Mentally Ill Inmates," *Boston Globe*, Sept. 13, 2016, https://www.bostonglobe.com/metro/2016/09/12/baker-plans-overhaul-criminal-justice-system-handling-mentally-ill/KIpXNF1YTfD81TEY1zWvjN/story.html.

THE GIFT THAT KEEPS ON GIVING: COLLATERAL CONSEQUENCES AND EXPANDED PUNISHMENTS

Howard Bailey was born in 1970 in Kingston, Jamaica. When he was just a young teenager, his mother left him and his siblings in Jamaica and legally immigrated to the United States, where she worked as a home health aide and saved up until she could afford to bring her family to the United States. Four years later, when he was seventeen, Bailey was finally able to immigrate legally to the United States, and to be reunited with his mother. He enrolled in high school and adjusted to his new life, meeting and befriending immigrants from all over the world at his Brooklyn school. When he graduated from high school, he enrolled in the Navy, proudly pledging, he explained, "to serve the country I now called home." He made it through boot camp, got assigned to a supply ship based in Norfolk, Virginia, and did two tours of duty in the Middle East during Operation Desert Storm. After four years, he decided he wanted to further his education, was honorably discharged, and enrolled in community college in Virginia, near the military base. He worked as a DJ spinning Caribbean tunes on a local radio show, met a woman, Judith, moved in with her, and eventually married her in 2001. They had one son together, Demique. By all accounts, Bailey was living the American Dream.

In the early 2000s, though, things went nightmarishly wrong. A Jamaican friend on the Norfolk military base asked if he could have some boxes from New York delivered to Bailey's house, instead of having them delivered to the military base. Bailey thought little of the seemingly reasonable request and agreed to help his friend out. When the boxes arrived—"each the size of a case of beer," Bailey remembered—he called his friend, asked where to take the packages, and made a plan to drop the boxes off with his friend after he dropped his son at school. As Bailey was driving into town, the police pulled him over. Those boxes turned out to be filled with marijuana, and were being tracked by the police. The Jamaican friend from the base disappeared and was never seen again. Bailey was arrested, pled guilty to possession of marijuana with intent to distribute (on the recommendation of his public defender), and was sentenced to the mandatory minimum term of fifteen months in a state work camp. While he was incarcerated, his wife Judith gave birth to their second child, a daughter, Jada. Their family made it through the tough period of his incarceration, his wife and daughter visiting him every weekend. When he was released, he was eager to support his family. He believed he had served his time, and he worked hard to put the experience behind him.[1]

This chapter begins with Howard Dean Bailey's post-prison odyssey of escalating *collateral consequences*—the lingering effects of his criminal conviction, or "legal sanctions and restrictions," which limited his ability to work, to have a family, and ultimately to continue to reside in the United States.[2] Collateral consequences are distinct from criminal punishments, like fines for speeding, or terms in prison. Fines and prison terms— sometimes called "direct consequences"—generally require certain legal procedures, like a hearing, and a right to appeal, before they can be imposed. A judge or jury imposes direct consequences. Collateral consequences, on the other hand, attach automatically, once a punishment has been assessed. Defendants need not even know that these consequences

---

[1] Howard Dean Bailey, "I Served My Country. Then It Kicked Me Out," *Politico Magazine*, Apr. 10, 2014, http://www.politico.com/magazine/story/2014/04/howard-dean-bailey -deported-i-served-my-country-and-then-it-kicked-me-out-105606?o=0.

[2] American Bar Association, "National Inventory of the Collateral Consequences of Conviction," 2012, http://www.abacollateralconsequences.org/. Note: this website provides an interactive map of U.S. jurisdictions, organized by state, and the collateral consequences of criminal convictions in each jurisdiction.

will attach before they plead guilty—just as Bailey did not know the long-term consequences of pleading guilty to the marijuana charge.[3]

Following Bailey's story, this chapter steps back to examine the history of these collateral consequences and their origins in an ancient legal concept of "civil death." The remainder of the chapter explains how, in the twenty-first century, these collateral consequences have expanded in both variety and duration of impact, attaching sometimes at the moment of arrest, and stretching out beyond an individual's death. Finally, the chapter explores the ripple effects of collateral consequences—beyond individuals—on families, communities, and institutions. As with abused prisoners' attempts to assert their rights and the attempts of imprisoned people with mental illness to get care while incarcerated, people managing the collateral consequences of criminal convictions struggle with both rendering harms visible and overcoming legal barriers to reform. Throughout, this chapter asks about the costs and benefits of collateral consequences, and about whether there are any limits on the scope and durations of the sanctions that attach as a result of a criminal record—and queries what limits, if any, should exist.

HOWARD DEAN BAILEY

Like many people with felony convictions, Bailey probably had difficulty finding work after he was released from that federal work camp.[4] First he took over a Caribbean restaurant, named it Caribbean Hut, and served "Caribbean and American junk food." Managing his own business likely spared him the need to go through a background check, in which he would have had to admit his prior conviction.[5] But the restaurant business was hard and kept him away from his family day and night. When a customer

---

[3] Jenny Roberts, "The Mythical Divide Between Collateral and Direct Consequences of Criminal Convictions: Involuntary Commitment of 'Sexually Violent Predators,'" *Minnesota Law Review* 93 (2008): 670–740, 672–3.

[4] See, e.g., Binyamin Appelbaum, "Out of Trouble, Out of Work," New York Times, Mar. 1, 2015: BU1; Devah Pager, *Marked: Race, Crime and Finding Work in an Era of Mass Incarceration* (Chicago: University of Chicago Press, 2007).

[5] See, e.g., "Employment Opportunities for Convicted Felons," Feb. 8, 2014, http://felonopportunities.com/employment-opportunities-for-convicted-felons/.

suggested trucking as a lucrative, stable job, Bailey pursued that opportunity, earning his truckers' license and investing in his own truck in 2003. At this point, Bailey finally felt like he had stable employment and could support his family. He could afford vacations to Disney World, and his kids were excelling in school, playing basketball and football, and joining him in the kitchen, sharing his love of cooking. He and his wife bought a house. The American Dream seemed alive again—so alive that Bailey applied for citizenship in 2005, to solidify his legal permanent resident status. On the citizenship form, he freely admitted his single prior conviction for possession of marijuana with intent to distribute. He had served his time and gotten on with his life, so he had no reason to think the earlier conviction would cause him any problems.

But months and then years went by without Bailey hearing anything about his citizenship application. He waited. And he waited. He would call and check on his application periodically, but he received no answers. He kept driving his truck, kept cooking with his kids, kept paying his mortgage. Eventually, he hired a lawyer to help him find out what was taking so long with his citizenship application. The attorney learned, after a meeting with immigration officials (agents within what is now called Immigrations and Customs Enforcement, or ICE), that the problem was something about obtaining documentation from the Virginia courts regarding the marijuana conviction. So Bailey kept waiting.

Then at the crack of dawn on June 10, 2010, there were loud knocks on his front door. Bailey jumped out of bed, and went to the door, still wearing his pajamas. As he opened the door, Bailey saw eleven immigration officials and state troopers, bulletproof vests donned, weapons drawn. They encircled Bailey, pushed him into his living room, and quickly cuffed him. His wife and young daughter rushed downstairs, screaming. They had no idea what was going on. Bailey had to beg to be permitted to put on pants, and his wife had to do it for him, while he remained cuffed. He did not know why he was even arrested until he arrived at the immigration building, where he had originally gone to apply for citizenship. He was locked into a detention cell there. And he learned that, because of his prior conviction, he was not only precluded from becoming a U.S. citizen, he was subject to automatic deportation. His citizenship application alerted Immigration and Customs Enforcement officials to his status and triggered his arrest.

Over the next two years, Bailey remained locked up in various detention facilities, trying to challenge his deportation. He explained that he had not known when he pled guilty to the marijuana charge that the guilty plea had immigration consequences. His lawyer had not known either—and even agreed to admit that he had not competently represented Bailey. But nothing worked.

Bailey was deported back to Jamaica in 2012. He had not been there in twenty years. He had no idea what to do to earn a living. His family sent him $1,500 to try to help him to start a pig farm, but a drought depleted his access to running water, and the business venture seemed on the verge of failing. After two years, his wife filed for divorce, because Bailey had no hope of returning to the United States. As of 2016, he had not seen his two U.S. citizen children in more than four years.[6]

A decades-old criminal conviction ended up ruining Bailey's career, tearing apart his family, and stripping him of residency rights. He had served his time, so how was this possible? While the specific details of the collateral consequences vary among citizens and noncitizens, according to the severities of the crime, and differences in sentencing from state to state, Bailey's experiences are common: his shock about the ongoing consequences of an old conviction; the fundamentally destructive impact of these consequences on Bailey, his family, and his community; and the hopelessness he now faces, without any opportunity to recover or redeem himself from his past actions.[7]

Bailey's story exemplifies the collateral consequences that many people with felony convictions face in the United States in the era of mass incarceration. As the number of people incarcerated in the United States has grown, so has the number of people released from prison, living in our communities, and haunted by their prior criminal records.

---

[6] Bailey, "I Served My Country."

[7] For a list of stories just like Bailey's, specifically describing deportations pursuant to old criminal convictions, see Immigrant Defense Project, "Immigrant Stories," http://www.immdefense.org/immigrant-stories/.

Many of them face ongoing civil rights limitations as a result of their criminal convictions, including prohibitions on voting, accessing public benefits, carrying guns, and even, as Bailey experienced, continuing to live in the United States.[8] Indeed, the scope and application of these restrictive laws have expanded simultaneously with mass incarceration over the last forty years.[9] The millions of people in the United States now living with criminal records—or being deported, like Bailey, because of such histories—represent yet another invisible aspect of mass incarceration. How did these collateral consequences of criminal convictions come into being, and how are they justified?

THE ORIGINS OF COLLATERAL CONSEQUENCES

The scale of mass incarceration in the United States, and a burgeoning range of associated sanctions, like the limitations on employment and residency that Bailey experienced, have recently brought attention to the phenomenon of collateral consequences. But the collateral sanctions associated with being convicted of a crime have existed as long as punishments have existed. In early Roman and Germanic tribal communities, societies subjected people convicted of crimes to "outlawry": they lost all rights to family (with spouses treated as widows and children as orphans), property, and even life (no one would be punished for killing the criminal). As political structures became more robust, so did the collateral consequences of crime. In ancient Greece and Rome, being convicted of a crime could lead not only to specific punishments but to permanent "infamy": the stripping of rights of citizenship, including rights to vote, speak publicly, serve in the army, or appear in court. In medieval Europe, convicted criminals faced "civil death"; although they might have remained alive in prison, they lost all rights to make contracts—for marriage, or property— and prior possessions were distributed as if the criminal had died. As early

[8] Marc Mauer and Meda Chesney-Lind, *Invisible Punishment: The Collateral Consequences of Mass Imprisonment* (New York: New Press, 2002).
[9] See, e.g., Chrysanthi Leon, *Sex Fiends, Perverts, and Pedophiles: Understanding Sex Crime Policy in America* (New York: New York University Press, 2011).

as the eighteenth century, though, European reformers criticized the idea of civil death (or *civiliter mortuus,* as discussed in Chapter One), and by the mid-nineteenth century, many countries had abolished it.[10]

In the United States, on the other hand, civil death-like provisions were built into state laws from the earliest days of the Republic. Legislators denied those convicted of crimes from entering contracts, maintaining marriages, participating in civil litigation, and accessing various government benefits. Prisoners also lost basic constitutional protections, like the right to a local jury trial—as described in Chapter One in the discussion of the 1871 case of *Ruffin v. Commonwealth.* In fact, after the Civil War, the Fourteenth Amendment enshrined another form of civil death in the U.S. Constitution: permitting states to deny the right to vote to those convicted of crimes (discussed further in Chapter Four). As late as the 1960s, a criminal conviction in the United States automatically resulted in the dissolution of a pre-existing marriage. In the 1960s, though, reformers advocated for limitations to these collateral consequences: reinstating civil rights for prisoners after they served their time; sealing, clearing, or expunging prior criminal records; and generally facilitating social re-integration. A study in the 1980s suggested collateral consequences had decreased substantially over the twentieth century. But such consequences began to expand again in the 1980s, in tandem with the expanding prison populations of mass incarceration.[11]

This long-standing American commitment to collateral consequences is surprising in light of early American history. After all, the United States began as a British colony, accepting (if not by choice) those with British criminal convictions whom the British government sent to start a new life

[10] For a review of this history, see Mirjan R. Damaska, "Adverse Legal Consequences of Conviction and Their Removal: A Comparative Study," *Journal of Criminal Law, Criminology, and Political Science* 59, no. 3 (1969): 347–60, 350–52. See also Jeremy Travis, "Invisible Punishment: An Instrument of Social Exclusion," in *Invisible Punishment: The Collateral Consequences of Mass Imprisonment,* Marc Mauer and Meda Chesney-Lind, eds. (New York: New Press, 2002), 15–36, 15–16.

[11] Nora V. Demleitner, "Preventing Internal Exile: The Need for Restrictions on Collateral Sentencing Consequences," *Stanford Law & Policy Review* 11, no. 1 (1999): 153–71, 154; see also Travis, "Invisible Punishment."

in America, free from outlawry, infamy, and civil death.[12] But the United States also began as a slaveholding nation, and scholars have consistently pointed to the complex relationship between slavery, punishment, and social control as an explanation for the U.S. attachment to civil death and collateral consequences.[13]

Specifically, when the United States abolished slavery during the Civil War, many Southern states imposed "Jim Crow" laws, which maintained racial segregation: requiring separate public facilities for blacks and whites and imposing onerous requirements, like taxes and literacy tests, to discourage blacks from voting. Importantly, these Jim Crow laws further excluded African-Americans from civil society by facilitating their criminalization. As early as the mid-nineteenth century, African-Americans were disproportionately among the incarcerated, especially in the South, and prisoners were frequently forced to work on plantation farms, making incarceration functionally comparable to slavery.[14] (And according to cases like *Ruffin v. Commonwealth*, discussed in Chapter One, courts considered prisoners to be, literally "slaves of the state.")

[12] See Demleitner, "Preventing Internal Exile."

[13] On civil and social death, see Orlando Patterson, *Slavery and Social Death: A Comparative Study* (Cambridge: Harvard University Press, 1982). For a discussion of how this plays out in the context of school discipline (and the connections to punishment), see Pedro A. Noguera, "Schools, Prisons, and Social Implications of Punishment: Rethinking Disciplinary Practices," *Theory into Practice* 42, no. 4 (2003): 341–50. On the relationship between slavery, the ghetto, and incarceration, see Loïc Wacquant, "Deadly Symbiosis," *Punishment and Society* 3, no. 1 (2001): 95–134.

[14] This system was known as "convict leasing." For two studies of the practice, see Matthew J. Mancini, *One Dies, Get Another: Convict Leasing in the American South, 1866–1928* (Charleston: University of South Carolina Press, 1996); Alex Lichtenstein, *Twice the Work of Free Labor: The Political Economy of Convict Labor in the New South* (New York: Verso, 1996). For a recent documentary exploring the relationship between antebellum slavery and modern criminal justice, see Ava DuVernay, *13th: A Netflix Original Documentary* (2016), and for a critique of this film, see Dan Berger, "Mass Incarceration And Its Mystification: A Review of the *13th*," *African-American Intellectual Historical Society*, Oct. 22, 2016, http://www.aaihs.org/mass-incarceration-and-its-mystification-a-review-of-the-13th/. For an explicit analysis of the links between collateral consequences and slavery, see Margaret Love, "Collateral Consequences a Legacy of Slavery," *Collateral Consequences Resource Center*, Jun. 25, 2015, http://ccresourcecenter.org/2015/06/25/collateral-consequences-a-legacy-of-slavery/.

Today, laws like those Bailey experienced, when he had difficulty finding a job and then was deported from the United States, are part of a network of laws often referred to as the "New Jim Crow," a term popularized by legal scholar Michelle Alexander. Alexander explains that a network of debilitating criminal laws and stigmatizing collateral consequences laws keep prisoners and former prisoners, all disproportionately men of color, from getting jobs, accessing social benefits, voting, serving on juries, or holding public office. This network of laws functions as an extension of those old, racially targeted, post—Civil War Jim Crow laws.[15] Alexander's analysis provides an important (if controversial[16]) paradigm for understanding both the historical roots of collateral consequences and the ongoing, systematic oppression these sanctions impose on former prisoners.

Whether or not collateral consequences are literally a new form of Jim Crow laws, they have distinctly disproportionate impacts on both racial minorities and lower income individuals. African-Americans, for instance, are more likely to have criminal records and to experience collateral consequences than white Americans. Half of all black males in the United States have been arrested at least once before they turn twenty-three.[17] And even an arrest can create a criminal record, with the many associated consequences described here. Just as prisoners tend to be less educated, less healthy, and less white than the average American, so do those experiencing the collateral consequences of arrest, conviction, and incarceration.[18]

---

[15] Michelle Alexander, *The New Jim Crow: Mass Incarceration in the Age of Colorblindness* (New York: New Press, 2012).

[16] For a critique of the New Jim Crow analogy, see James Forman, "Racial Critiques of Mass Incarceration: Beyond the New Jim Crow," *New York University Law Review* 87 (2012): 101–46.

[17] Robert Brame, Shawn D. Bushway, Ray Paternoster, and Michael G. Turner, "Demographic Patterns of Cumulative Arrest Prevalence by Ages 18 and 23," *Crime and Delinquency* 60, no. 3 (2014): 471–86.

[18] See Keramet Reiter, "Making Windows in Walls: Strategies for Prison Research," *Qualitative Inquiry* 20, no. 4: 417–28; for a survey of the various disparate impacts of collateral consequences, see also Michael Pinard, "Collateral Consequences of Criminal Convictions: Confronting Issues of Race and Dignity," *New York University Law Review* 85 (2010): 457–534, 511–17.

THE SCOPE OF COLLATERAL CONSEQUENCES

The preceding sections have provided a basic working definition of what constitutes a collateral consequence, illustrated some of the individual impacts of collateral consequences, and contextualized their history. But how many kinds of collateral consequences exist, and how widespread are they? As it turns out, those questions are surprisingly difficult to answer—for two reasons.

First, collateral consequences elude detection, in multiple ways. As Bailey found out the hard way, collateral consequences are invisible at imposition, attaching automatically with a criminal sentence, rather than deliberatively by decision of a judge or jury. Collateral consequences are also often fairly hidden at inception, too. Unlike sentencing schemes, which legislators and voters usually debate publicly, and which judiciary committees review, collateral consequences are often attached as piecemeal afterthoughts in legislation at both the state and federal level, producing complex interactions between convictions and sanctions across different jurisdictions.[19] For instance, Bailey was convicted of the state crime of marijuana possession, but then faced the federal (or national) consequence of deportation.

Second, the sheer variation of collateral consequences from crime to crime, county to county, and state to state makes them difficult to catalogue.[20] Certain consequences attach to certain kinds of arrests, crimes, or punishments, and different counties, states, and federal agencies have different rules about what consequences are associated with what crimes. There is so much variety, in fact, that agencies across the United States have been working to better identify and track the range of collateral consequences that exist today. The American Bar Association now maintains a website, funded by the National Institute of Justice, which attempts to document these collateral consequences by jurisdiction. To date, the

[19] See Travis, "Invisible Punishment," 16–17.
[20] Sarah B. Berson, "Beyond the Sentence: Understanding Collateral Consequences," *NIJ Journal*, 272 (2013): 25–28, http://www.nij.gov/journals/272/pages/collateral-consequences.aspx.

website identifies 44,500 different collateral consequences laws across the United States.[21]

The American Bar Association website inventorying collateral consequences lists sanctions by state, and catalogues hundreds of such consequences in each state. The consequences can, broadly, be divided into positive and negative legal obligations. *Positive obligations* require people with criminal records to do certain things, depending on the prior conviction. For instance, some people are required to pay fees associated with their prior arrest, crime, or punishment; to register as sex offenders wherever they live; or to submit to certain kinds of drug or behavioral treatments. *Negative obligations*, or exclusions, prevent people with criminal records from doing certain things, like living in public housing; receiving welfare; receiving government loans to support the pursuit of education; voting; or, as in Bailey's case, living in the United States. Some of the obligations and exclusions imposed on those with criminal convictions have immediate effects on families. For instance, sometimes parental rights to children are terminated during a parent's incarceration, or sometimes the parent of a juvenile convicted of a crime is obligated to pay the fines and fees originally assigned to the juvenile (as discussed in the next section).

Both the positive obligations and the negative exclusions affect nearly every category of rights and privileges: social, economic, and political.[22] While a criminal conviction no longer results in the automatic dissolution of a marriage, as it did in the United States just a few decades ago, it can result in plenty of other social losses, from lack of access to financial supports (through exclusion from government assistance programs) to naming and shaming (through posting public notices of criminal activity, as on sex offender registries). Economically, a criminal conviction can disqualify a person from all kinds of

---

[21] See http://www.abacollateralconsequences.org/. For a quiz to test your basic knowledge of collateral consequences, see Christie Thompson, "How Can a Criminal Record Haunt You for the Rest of Your Life?" *The Marshall Project*, Oct. 2, 2016, https://www.themarshallproject.org/2016/10/02/how-can-a-criminal-record-haunt-you-for-the-rest-of-your-life?utm_medium=email&utm_campaign=newsletter&utm_source=opening-statement&utm_term=newsletter-20161003-598#.JO9ECRm1i.

[22] Pinard, "Collateral Consequences," 460; Demleitner, "Preventing Internal Exile," 356–60.

employment and licensing opportunities—from serving in the military to earning a cosmetology license.[23] And politically, a criminal conviction can disqualify a person from voting, serving on a jury, or holding public office.[24] (Note that this chapter focuses in on the social and economic consequences of criminal convictions, and Chapter Four revisits the political consequences.)

Both the invisibility and the variability of collateral consequences begins to explain how Bailey's original defense lawyer in his marijuana possession case did not know the potential collateral consequences of his client's guilty plea. Absent a resource like the National Inventory of the Collateral Consequences of Conviction (which was only initiated in 2012), people like Howard Dean Bailey are all the more likely to have no idea about the potential consequences of a criminal conviction, and therefore to be unable to make a reasonable decision about whether and when to plead guilty to a crime in the first place, or how to move forward with their lives, beyond the sentence served for that crime.

Moreover, the wide range of tangible legal obligations and exclusions attaching to people like Bailey amplifies the less tangible stigma that attaches to those with criminal convictions, even absent collateral consequences. Specifically, quantitative sociologists have noted that the simple fact of having a criminal record can decrease the chances of a successful job application by 50 percent for white applicants and by as much as 64 percent for African-American applicants. Qualitative sociologists have described how people with criminal records feel stigmatized and unable to be fully reintegrated members of society.[25] This stigma compounds the disadvantage that tends to characterize former prisoners and people with criminal records, including: higher rates of mental illness (as discussed in Chapter Two); higher rates of addiction and of infectious and chronic

---

[23] For a list of federal disqualifications, see *Federal Statutes Imposing Collateral Consequences Upon Conviction* (Washington D.C.: U.S. Department of Justice, Nov. 13, 2006), http://ccresourcecenter.org/2015/06/25/collateral-consequences-a-legacy-of-slavery/.

[24] See Demleitner, "Preventing Internal Exile," 356–60; *Federal Statutes*.

[25] Pager, *Marked*; Shadd Maruna, "Reentry as a Rite of Passage," *Punishment & Society* 13, no.1 (2013): 3–27. For a thorough review of the literature on the stigma—both tangible and intangible—attaching to criminal convictions, see James Jacobs, *The Eternal Criminal Record* (Cambridge: Harvard University Press, 2015).

diseases; and lower rates of literacy and education than the general U.S. population.[26]

Criminologist John Braithwaite distinguishes between the stigmatizing, or disintegrative, shame associated with a traditional criminal conviction and what he calls the *reintegrative* shame associated with a restorative justice model of punishment. Restorative justice models respect individual autonomy and acknowledge wrong actions, while also forgiving and re-incorporating individuals back into the community.[27] The model of reintegrative shaming, or restorative justice, however, is not what is currently driving the system of collateral consequences in the United States. People like Howard Dean Bailey, for instance, have lost all hope of re-integration.

Instead, millions of people across the United States (and millions of others, like Bailey, who have been excluded from the United States entirely) are affected by collateral consequences that further stigmatize and exacerbate the disintegrative shame associated with criminal convictions. Each year, approximately 650,000 people are released from prisons across the United States, and millions more cycle through jails.[28] This means that more than half a million people annually join the list of those eligible

[26] For a survey of the physical health problems prisoners face, see Ingrid A. Bingswanger, "Chronic Medical Diseases Among Jail and Prison Inmates," American College of Correctional Physicians, Mar. 3, 2010, http://societyofcorrectionalphysicians.org/corrdocs/corrdocs-archives/winter-2010/chronic-medical-diseases-among-jail-and-prison-inmates. According to the Prison Policy Initiative, 19 percent of the U.S. prison population is completely illiterate, and 40 percent are "functionally illiterate," which means being would be "unable to write a letter explaining a billing error." Peter Wagner, "The Prison Index: Taking the Pulse of the Crime Control Industry" (Northampton: Prison Policy Initiative, 2003), http://www.prisonpolicy.org/prisonindex/rootsofcrime.html. An updated analysis of prison literacy should be available in 2017 here: https://nces.ed.gov/naal/prison_lit.asp. For a discussion of the many challenges prisoners face upon re-entry, as a result of these many forms of disadvantage, see the series of reports produced by the Urban Institute as part of the *Returning Home Study: Understanding the Challenges of Prisoner Re-entry*, available online here: http://www.urban.org/policy-centers/justice-policy-center/projects/returning-home-study-understanding-challenges-prisoner-reentry.

[27] See John Braithwaite, *Crime, Shame and Reintegration* (Cambridge: Cambridge University Press, 1989).

[28] Peter Wagner and Bernadette Rabuy, *Mass Incarceration: The Whole Pie 2016* (Northampton: Prison Policy Initiative 2016), http://www.prisonpolicy.org/reports/pie2016.html. See also "Prisonersand Prisoner Re-Entry," U.S. Department of Justice, https://www.justice.gov/archive/fbci/progmenu_reentry.html.

to experience the collateral consequences described here. Estimates are that at least 100 million Americans have a criminal record. That's one in every three Americans—at least as many as have a college degree.[29]

As the United States enters its fourth decade of mass incarceration, and the effects of the collateral consequences of having a criminal conviction reach one in three Americans, there are now collateral consequences to the collateral consequences. The social, economic, and political restrictions affecting people who have been convicted of a crime are now starting to have significant impacts on noncriminals, including: the children and parents of the convicted, the broader communities where people with criminal records return and attempt to rebuild their lives in the face of so many challenges and barriers, and even the legal actors working within a system of compromised rights and privileges. The following sections explore these broader impacts of collateral consequences, raising questions about whether these affects on families, communities, and institutions are either fair or socially productive. Consider whether the scope of these consequences furthers any of the possible goals of punishment, from deterrence to restoration?

FAMILIAL COLLATERAL: PERPETUAL POVERTY

More than half of prisoners in the United States are parents to children under the age of 18.[30] An estimated 2 million U.S. children have an incarcerated parent at any given time, and as many as 10 million have had

---

[29] William Sabol, *Survey of State Criminal History Information Systems, 2012* (Washington, D.C.: U.S. Department of Justice, Bureau of Justice Statistics, Jan. 2014), https://www .ncjrs.gov/pdffiles1/bjs/grants/244563.pdf.Forpowerfulvisualizationsofthesenumbers, see *Americans with Criminal Records* (Washington, D.C.: The Sentencing Project, 2015), http://www.sentencingproject.org/wp-content/uploads/2015/11/Americans-with-Criminal-Records-Poverty-and-Opportunity-Profile.pdf; Rebecca Vallas and Sharon Dietrich, *One Strike and You're Out: How We Can Eliminate Barriers to Economic Security and Mobility for People with Criminal Records* (Washington, D.C.: Center for American Progress, 2014), https://cdn.americanprogress.org/wp-content/uploads /2014/12/VallasCriminalRecordsReport.pdf.

[30] *Americans with Criminal Records.*

a parent incarcerated at some point during their childhood.[31] These children are more likely to live in poverty, experience household instability, underperform academically, and suffer an array of behavioral problems compared to children who do not have incarcerated parents.[32] The magnitude of harm children experience when a parent is incarcerated, in fact, is comparable to being abused or experiencing domestic violence.[33]

Parent-child contact is often severely curtailed during incarceration. Half of incarcerated parents never receive personal visits from their children during their incarceration.[34] Even phone calls can be difficult to make and expensive (as detailed in Chapter Five). And many parents will have their parental rights terminated during their incarceration, as a collateral consequence of the incarceration.

In 1997, President Clinton signed the Adoption and Safe Families Act, which required states to terminate the parental rights of children who had been in foster care for fifteen of the prior twenty-two months. Median sentences in the United States are significantly longer than fifteen months. So parents without access to substitute care for their children—like a

---

[31] "Children of Incarcerated Parents Fact Sheet," Osborne Association, http://www .osborneny.org/images/uploads/printMedia/Initiative%20CIP%20Stats_Fact%20 Sheet.pdf; *Collateral Costs: Incarceration's Effect on Economic Mobility* (Washington, D.C.: The Pew Charitable Trusts, Pew Center on the States, 2010), http://www.pewtrusts. org/~/media/legacy/uploadedfiles/pcs_assets/2010/collateralcosts1pdf.pdf.

[32] For studies of the effects on children of parental incarceration, see Sara Wakefield and Chris Wildeman, *Children of the Prison Boom* (New York: Oxford University Press, 2003). See also A. Geller, I. Garfinkel, C. E. Cooper, and R. Mincy, "Parental Incarceration and Childhood Well-Being: Implications for Urban Families," *Social Science Quarterly* 90 (2009): 1186–1202; A. Haskins, "Unintended Consequences: Effects of Paternal Incarceration On Child School Readiness and Later Special Education Placement," *Sociological Science* 1 (2014): 141–58; Chris Wildeman and Kristin Turney, "Positive, Negative, or Null? the Effects of Maternal Incarceration On Children's Behavioral Problems," *Demography* 51, no. 3 (2014): 1041–68.

[33] *A Shared Sentence: The Devastating Toll of Parental Incarceration on Kids, Families, and Communities* (Baltimore: Annie E. Casey Foundation, Apr. 2016), http://www.aecf .org/m/resourcedoc/aecf-asharedsentence-2016.pdf.

[34] Sarah Schirmer, Ashley Nellis, and Marc Mauer, *Incarcerated Parents and Their Children: Trends, 1991–2007* (Washington, D.C.: The Sentencing Project, 2009), http://www .sentencingproject.org/wp-content/uploads/2016/01/Incarcerated-Parents-and -Their-Children-Trends-1991-2007.pdf. For an in-depth report on the experience of parent-child visitation in Georgia prisons, see Craig Schneider, "When Mom is in Prison," *Atlanta Journal-Constitution*, Oct. 17, 2016, http://specials.myajc.com/mom-prison/.

grandparent or spouse—are likely to loose their parental rights over the course of their incarceration.[35] Policies dissolving parental rights create further collateral consequences upon re-entry; former prisoners without strong familial attachments have higher unemployment rates and higher substance abuse rates than former prisoners with stronger attachments.[36]

For women prisoners who give birth while incarcerated, the collateral consequences are even more immediate, and severe. Across the United States, women who give birth in prison are shackled during the birth, and then have their babies forcibly removed from them forty-eight hours after birth. In spite of public outcry against a practice condemned as a human rights violation, twenty-eight states still permit the shackling of women during childbirth.[37] The experience can hardly be better for the newborn than for the mother.

In eight (of one hundred) women's prisons in the United States, a select few mothers are allowed to keep their newborn babies with them during their incarceration. The smallest mistake—in the mother's behavior, or in her treatment of the child—can result in revocation of the privilege of cohabitation, however. The practice is more common in other countries, from South Sudan to France, Denmark, and other European countries, which all have laws requiring that mothers and babies be permitted to stay together.[38]

Even for those parents who are able to maintain contact with their kids and regain custody upon release from prison, tens of thousands will be

[35] Patricia E. Allard and Lynn D. Lu, *Rebuilding Families, Reclaiming Lives: State Obligations to Children in Foster Care and Their Incarcerated Parents* (New York: The Brennan Center for Justice, 2006), http://www.brennancenter.org/sites/default/files/legacy/d/download_file_37203.pdf.

[36] Nancy G. La Vigne, Tracey Lloyd, and Sara Debus-Sherrill, *One Year Out: Tracking the Experiences of Male Prisoners Returning to Houston, Texas* (Washington, D.C.: The Urban Institute, 2009), http://www.urban.org/research/publication/one-year-out-tracking-experiences-male-prisoners-returning-houston-texas/view/full_report.

[37] Collier Meyerson, "The Shocking Practice Pregnant Women Endure in American Prisons," *Fusion*, Oct. 12, 2015, http://fusion.net/story/212720/the-shocking-practice-pregnant-women-endure-in-american-prisons/; "The Shackling of Pregnant Women & Girls in U.S. Prisons, Jails & Youth Detention Centers," ACLU National Prison Project Briefing Paper, https://www.aclu.org/files/assets/anti-shackling_briefing_paper_stand_alone.pdf.

[38] Darren Boyle, "Raised Behind Bars," *Daily Mail*, May 25, 2016, http://www.dailymail.co.uk/news/article-3608322/Born-bars-Inside-America-s-maximum-security-prisons-babies-stay-felon-mothers-serve-jail-sentences.html.

ineligible for public assistance, and hundreds of thousands will be unable to find jobs to help support their families. Almost 200,000 women are subject to *lifetime* bans from public assistance because of prior convictions. And among formerly incarcerated individuals of both genders, 60 percent are unemployed one year after they are released from prison. For those lucky enough to find employment, the jobs tend to be short-term and low-paying—40 percent lower-paying than jobs acquired by similarly situated people without criminal records.[39]

Parents of incarcerated kids also face their own collateral consequences. On any given day, there are at least 50,000 children incarcerated in the United States.[40] When collateral consequences of convictions attach to these kids, their parents often suffer at least as much. Take Maria Rivera's story. In 2008, her son was arrested in Orange County; California, he was sentenced to almost two years in juvenile detention. (His record is sealed, so his crime is unknown.[41]) In 2010, Rivera's son was released from juvenile detention, and Orange County sent Rivera a bill for $16,372: $23.90 per day for each day of her son's incarceration, and $2,199 for his legal expenses.[42]

In one sense, this was a classic collateral consequence of incarceration: a punishment not directly imposed by a judge or a jury, but instead automatically attaching as a result of Rivera's son's sentence. In another sense, though, this was an unusual collateral consequence of incarceration: imposed not on the convicted criminal but directly on a family member.

[39] Ibid. See also H. J. Holzer, S. Raphael, and M. A. Stoll, "Will Employers Hire Former Offenders? Employer Preferences, Background Checks, and Their Determinants," in M. Pattillo, B. Western, and D. Weiman, eds., *Imprisoning America: The Social Effects of Mass Incarceration* (New York: Russell Sage Foundation, 2004): 205–43; Devah Pager, "The Mark of a Criminal Record," *American Journal of Sociology* 108, no. 5 (2003): 937–75; Sara Wakefield and Christopher Uggen, "Incarceration and Stratification," *Annual Review of Sociology* 36 (2010): 387–406.

[40] "Statistical Briefing Book: Juveniles in Corrections: Demographics," Office of Juvenile Justice and Delinquency Prevention 2016, https://www.ojjdp.gov/ojstatbb/corrections/qa08201.asp?qaDate=2014.

[41] Jordan Graham, "Mom Goes Bankrupt Paying for Son's Incarceration, Court Scolds O.C. for Pursuit of Debt," *Orange County Register*, Aug. 19, 2016, http://www.ocregister.com/articles/county-726412-rivera-bankruptcy.html.

[42] *Rivera v. Orange County Probation Department*, 832 F. 3d 1103 (9th Cir. 2016), https://cdn.ca9.uscourts.gov/datastore/opinions/2016/08/10/14-60044.pdf.

Maria Rivera accepted full responsibility for this bill, although she had little means to pay it. She immediately sold her house, which allowed her to pay $9,508—more than half of what she owed. At this point, Rivera lost the ability to provide stable housing for herself and her son.[43] This is especially ironic given the strong relationship, established in sociological and policy research, between ongoing familial support and successful reentry from prison back into communities—in terms of lower recidivism rates and higher employment rates, for instance.[44] The collateral fees Rivera was assessed produced further and worse collateral consequences.

And still the county continued to send bills to Rivera, alleging she still owed $9,908—almost $3,000 more than the balance she should have owed based on her initial payment. An Orange County court entered a default judgment against Rivera. She filed for bankruptcy. She had no assets. The bankruptcy court granted her a "full discharge" and "fresh start."[45]

But Orange County probation officials fought the order—for five more years. They argued that the $9,908 bill they had sent to Rivera constituted a "domestic support obligation," akin to child support, and so could not be discharged, or avoided, through bankruptcy proceedings. Rivera went back to the bankruptcy court for help enforcing the order to discharge her debts, but the court agreed with county officials that Rivera still owed that $9,908 as a domestic support obligation. Rivera appealed the bankruptcy judge's decision—first to an appellate bankruptcy judge (the next level of review), and then to the Ninth Circuit Court of Appeals. There, someone finally took Rivera's side. Judge Reinhardt discharged the debt once and for all, with a few harsh words for the Orange County Probation Department, which had tried so hard to collect the debt:

> Orange County's persistence in collecting a debt of over $9,000 from a bankrupt woman who has acted in good faith in difficult circumstances has been nothing if not resolute. Rivera's case is troubling, however, because the County's

[43] *Rivera v. Orange County.*

[44] See the Urban Institute *Returning Home Study.*

[45] *Rivera v. Orange County,* 4.

> actions compromise the goals of juvenile correction and the
> best interests of the child, and, ironically, impair the ability of
> his mother to provide him with future support.[46]

Rivera's experience was far from unique; a California statute permits any county probation department to charge parents up to $30 per day for the reasonable costs of supporting a minor in detention.[47]

The University of California, Berkeley Policy Advocacy Clinic published a report just a few months before the decision in the *Rivera* case dubbing California's juvenile detention fee policies "high pain, no gain." The report noted that the policies disproportionately impacted families of color and exaggerated existing problems with economic and social instability.[48] Worse, the programs are not profitable; in fact, they tend to cost Californians money. In Contra Costa County (in Northern California), for instance, the Probations Collection Unit cost $500,000 per year to operate, but only collected $230,000 per year in revenue.[49]

The tens of thousands of dollars billed to mothers like Maria Rivera, just like the economic and social instability produced by parental incarceration, have immediate impacts on families. But familial instability, high unemployment rates, and insurmountable debt have impacts on communities, too.

COMMUNITY COLLATERAL: MILLION DOLLAR BLOCKS

One of the most vivid analogies for understanding the effects of collateral consequences on communities is "million dollar blocks." Eric Cadora coined the term in the early 2000s when he was working for the

[46] Ibid., 18.

[47] Cal. Welf. & Inst. Code § 903(a).

[48] *High Pain, No Gain: How Juvenile Administrative Fees Harm Low-Income Families in Alameda County, California* (Berkeley: University of California, Berkeley Law, Policy and Advocacy Clinic, March 2016), http://64.166.146.245/docs/2016/BOS/20161025_813/27510_PAC%20High%20Pain%2C%20No%20Gain.pdf.

[49] Gillian Edevane, "Contra Costa County Halts Fees for Parents of Juvenile Offenders," *NBC Bay Area*, Oct. 26, 2016, http://www.nbcbayarea.com/news/local/Contra-Costa -County-Halts-Fees-for-the-Parents-of-Juvenile-Offenders--398739671.html.

Open Society Institute, a philanthropic agency founded by billionaire businessman George Soros. Cadora used mapping software called GIS (Geographic Information System) to examine rates of incarceration by neighborhood, and he identified a series of million dollar blocks across the United States: urban neighborhoods with highly concentrated rates of incarceration. In these blocks, residents experience incarceration at significantly higher rates than in the overall city or state population.[50] Like the collateral consequences of incarceration that the American Bar Association has worked to catalogue and count, these million dollar blocks were largely invisible until Cadora found a way to literally put them on the map.

Cadora's website, called "Justice Mapping," provides just a few examples of how community experiences of incarceration are concentrated within these million dollar blocks scattered across the United States. For instance, *half* of all the people admitted to prison annually from New York City come from just a few neighborhoods that are home to less than *one-fifth* of the city's overall population. And *one-quarter* of all the people on probation and parole in Wichita, Kansas, are concentrated in fewer than *one-tenth* of the city's neighborhoods.[51]

In economic terms, this means that local and state governments spend millions of dollars per year incarcerating individuals from just a few neighborhoods—neighborhoods where the average income level tends to be at or below the poverty line. In Pennsylvania, for instance, state taxpayers spend $40 million per year to imprison residents from a single zip code in Philadelphia. In that zip code, nearly half of residents earn less than $25,000 per year, hovering just above the federal poverty line.[52] (Cadora's Justice Mapping website also contains interactive maps allowing visitors to examine million dollar blocks in their communities.[53])

---

[50] *Ending Mass Incarceration: Charting a New Justice Reinvestment*, (Washington, D.C.: The Sentencing Project, 2015), http://sentencingproject.org/wp-content/uploads/2015/12/Ending-Mass-Incarceration-Charting-a-New-Justice-Reinvestment.pdf.

[51] "Justice Mapping Center Launches First National Atlas of Criminal Justice Data," *Justice Mapping Center*, Oct. 5, 2010, http://www.justicemapping.org/archive/26/multi-%E2%80%98million-dollar%E2%80%99-blocks-of-brownsville/.

[52] "Justice Mapping Center Launches."

[53] See http://www.justiceatlas.org/.

Concentrated incarceration rates in certain neighborhoods mean: concentrated vulnerability to the kinds of fees and fines Maria Rivera faced when her son was incarcerated; concentrated unemployment as a result of prior criminal records; and concentrated familial instability as kids experience parental incarceration—or even parental deportation, as in the case of Howard Dean Bailey. The term million dollar blocks, then, highlights the irony of states spending millions of taxpayer dollars enforcing policies that ultimately exaggerate poverty and social problems in a few communities, which lacked resources in the first place. Cadora and colleagues have argued that one way to counteract the effects of million dollar blocks is to engage in "justice reinvestment," redirecting millions, and sometimes billions of dollars from incarceration to alternatives like treatment, diversion, and job training.[54]

Nonetheless, many communities have ignored (or distorted) these recommendations, instead imposing additional fines, fees, and taxes, directly tied to interactions with the criminal justice system, on the individuals residing in these million dollar blocks. Brett Story, a scholar who approaches prison studies from a geographic perspective, has recently argued that the very concept of the million dollar block functionally demonizes poor, racialized urban spaces. Story explains that, through the concept of the million-dollar block: "High concentrations of prisoners are . . . equated seamlessly with the problem of crime and violence, rather than, say, spatially uneven policing practices."[55] The resulting "justice reinvestment" policies encourage state intervention and concentrate social, racial, and crime controls within million dollar blocks. These policies have inspired social unrest in a number of these communities, where citizens joined together to protest and resist the network of violence and oppression trapping them in million dollar blocks. Ferguson, Missouri was one such flashpoint.

Ferguson, Missouri, as a town, looks something like a bloated version of one of Cadora's million dollar blocks. The demographics of the once

[54] See *Ending Mass Incarceration*; Todd R. Clear, John R. Hamilton, and Eric Cadora, *Community Justice*, 2nd ed. (New York: Routledge, 2010).

[55] See Brett Story, "The Prison in the City: Tracking the Neoliberal Life of the 'Million Dollar Block,'" *Theoretical Criminology* 20, no. 3 (2016): 257–76.

majority-white city were reversed within two decades, beginning in the 1990s. By 2014, 67 percent of the residents were African-American. And a full quarter lived below the federal poverty line—earning less than $16,000 per year per family of two.[56] Ferguson and its surrounding areas (near St. Louis) have some of the highest incarceration rates in the state of Missouri.[57]

On Saturday, August 9, 2014, Darren Wilson, a white, twenty-eight-year-old police officer, fired twelve bullets at Michael Brown, in the middle of a Ferguson street, in broad daylight. Brown was eighteen years old, unarmed, and black. He died quickly.

As news of the shooting spread, the entire city erupted in protest. Some of the protests were peaceful, others involved looting, and still others involved direct confrontations with the police. The unrest lasted for two weeks, and resurged in response to various state and federal officials' decisions to decline to prosecute officer Darren Wilson, and on anniversaries of Brown's death.[58]

Following Brown's death, and the unrest in Ferguson, the U.S. Department of Justice (DOJ) opened both a criminal investigation into officer Darren Wilson's actions and a civil investigation into the "patterns and practices" of the operation of the Ferguson Police Department. Although the DOJ ultimately declined to individually prosecute Wilson, they condemned the racist, predatory policing practices of the entire Ferguson police department.

Specifically, the DOJ's civil rights investigation uncovered how city, police, and court officials collaborated to maximize the fine and fee

[56] *Investigation of the Ferguson Police Department* (Washington, D.C.: U.S. Department of Justice, Civil Rights Division, Mar. 4, 2015): 6, https://www.justice.gov/sites/default/files/opa/press-releases/attachments/2015/03/04/ferguson_police_department_report.pdf.

[57] George A. Lombardi, "A Profile of the Institutional and Supervised Offender Population on June 30, 2012" (Jefferson City: Missouri Department of Corrections, 2013): 10, https://doc.mo.gov/Documents/publications/Offender%20Profile%20FY12.pdf.

[58] See "Timeline: The Death of Michael Brown and Unrest in Ferguson," *CBS St. Louis*, Aug. 12, 2014, http://stlouis.cbslocal.com/2014/08/12/timeline-the-death-of-michael-brown-and-unrest-in-ferguson/; "Q&A: What Happened in Ferguson?" *New York Times*, Aug. 10, 2015, http://www.nytimes.com/interactive/2014/08/13/us/ferguson-missouri-town-under-siege-after-police-shooting.html.

revenues accruing in the city's coffers. In 2015, $3 million, or nearly one quarter of the city's general revenues, came from collections of fines and fees associated with municipal violations, arrests, convictions, and other interactions with the criminal justice system.[59] In many cases, these fines and fees lacked any legal justification. Ferguson police tended to arrest people simply for being disrespectful. They frequently enforced a municipal statute prohibiting "failure to comply," which the DOJ found to be unconstitutional both in how it was written and in its enforcement. Ferguson police used the statute to compel people to identify themselves to police officers—a violation of the constitutionally guaranteed right to walk away from police encounters without answering questions, absent a formal detention or arrest.[60]

When individuals could not afford to pay an initial ticket or fine, for a violation like "failure to comply," Ferguson courts refused to provide alternative payment options. Instead, they levied additional fees and fines, issued warrants for arrest, and even jailed citizens for unpaid fines.

Black citizens bore a grossly disproportionate burden of the ticketing and fining. African Americans accounted for roughly 90 percent of all traffic stops, citations, and arrests between 2012 and 2014 in Ferguson, although they accounted for only about two-thirds of the municipal population.[61]

The DOJ concluded that Ferguson's policies did not just impact the individuals and families subjected to unconstitutional policing and insurmountable debt, but the policies also impacted the broader communities in which this debt was concentrated. "Ferguson law enforcement practices erode community trust, especially among Ferguson's African-American residents, and make policing less effective, more difficult, and less safe."[62] In other words, the DOJ investigation directly linked the exorbitant fines and fees assessed in Ferguson to the systemic social unrest the city had experienced in the wake of Michael Brown's shooting and death.

---

[59] *Investigation of the Ferguson Police Department*, 10.
[60] Ibid., 19–22.
[61] Ibid., 4.
[62] Ibid., 79.

Based on this conclusion, the DOJ ordered numerous changes to policing policies and practices in Ferguson.[63]

While Brown's death brought public attention and DOJ scrutiny to the unconstitutional pattern and practice of law enforcement in Ferguson, Missouri, that town is merely one of hundreds of cities in the United States where million dollar blocks, which cost tax payers millions in incarceration costs, have also become million dollar revenue generators for local municipalities and private debt collection agencies. The *Washington Post* reported in 2014 that many of the municipalities surrounding Ferguson, Missouri collected 40 percent or more of their annual income from fines and fees.[64] Just a few months before Michael Brown's death and the eruption of protests in Ferguson, the *New Yorker* ran a feature story about similar debt collection practices in Alabama. There, citizens who could not immediately pay traffic fines and nuisance violations entered a spiral of growing debt, subject to steep interest rates and fees from private collection agencies contracting with courts. As debts became insurmountable, citizens faced arrest warrants and jail time—all for an inability to pay a simple parking ticket.[65] Alexes Harris's recent book, poignantly titled *A Pound of Flesh*, details similar downward debt spirals in Washington state, and traces how these debt cycles reinforce racial and economic inequalities in entire communities.[66] Such practices are especially disturbing in light of the research

[63] These reforms were ordered during President Obama's administration, under the supervision of Attorney General Eric Holder. As of 2017, President Trump's new Attorney General, Jefferson Session, has threatened to stop enforcing these reforms. *See* Jelani Cobb, "Will Jeff Sessions Police the Police?" *New Yorker*, Apr. 24, 2017, http://www.newyorker.com/magazine/2017/04/24/will-jeff-sessions-police-the-police.

[64] Radley Balko, "How Municipalities in St. Louis County, Mo., Profit from Poverty," *Washington Post*, Sept. 3, 2014, https://www.washingtonpost.com/news/the-watch/wp/2014/09/03/how-st-louis-county-missouri-profits-from-poverty/?utm_term=.818d2e377bb8.

[65] Sarah Stillman, "Get Out of Jail, Inc.," *New Yorker*, Jun. 23, 2014, http://www.newyorker.com/magazine/2014/06/23/get-out-of-jail-inc.

[66] Alexes Harris, *A Pound of Flesh* (New York: Russell Sage Foundation, 2016). For another careful analysis of the impact of these policies on both families and communities, see Ta-Nehisi Coates, "The Black Family in the Age of Mass Incarceration," *Atlantic Monthly*, Oct. 2015, http://www.theatlantic.com/magazine/archive/2015/10/the-black-family-in-the-age-of-mass-incarceration/403246/. For other analyses of the impact of debt on re-entry, see Wendy Sawyer, *Punishing Poverty: The High Cost of Probation Fees in Massachusetts* (Northhampton: Prison Policy Initiative, 2016),

discussed throughout this chapter, which suggests that people with criminal records (including both prior arrests and prior incarcerations) have a more difficult time finding employment and earning even a minimum wage than people without criminal records.

Monetary sanctions imposed for criminalized activity, however, are not always so onerous as those imposed on communities in Missouri, Alabama, and Washington. Sometimes, such sanctions are imposed on *white-collar criminals*, who are easily able to escape the cycle of collateral consequences—debt, inability to pay, acquisition of criminal record, further inability to pay, mounting debt—that faced so many Ferguson residents. Scholars generally define white-collar crime as either (1) crime committed by people of high social status and respect, or (2) acts associated with particular actors' professions, or (3) some combination of these two kinds of criminals and criminal acts.[67] Examining white-collar crime reveals another form of disparity in the criminal justice system: some law breakers have better access to lawyers to defend their interests and resources to pay off fines immediately.[68] White-collar crimes, in other words, are one facet of a phenomenon known as "white advantage" in the criminal justice system. On the flip side of the harsh penalties experienced in predominantly African-American communities, like Ferguson, are lax penalties in predominantly white (and male) communities, like investment banks.

In fact, at the same time that DOJ lawyers were investigating Ferguson law enforcement officials and the fines and fees being imposed on some of the poorest Ferguson residents, they were also investigating some of the

https://www.prisonpolicy.org/probation/ma_report.html; Karin D. Martin, Sandra Susan Smith, and Wendy Still, *Shackled to Debt: Criminal Justice Financial Obligations and the Barriers to Re-Entry They Create* (Washington, D.C.: National Institute of Justice, 2017), https://www.ncjrs.gov/pdffiles1/nij/249976.pdf.

[67] E. H. Sutherland, "White-Collar Criminality," *American Sociological Review* 5 (1940): 1–12; Sally S. Simpson, "White-Collar Crime: A Review of Recent Developments and Promising Directions for Future Research," *Annual Review of Sociology* 39 (2013): 309–31.

[68] For a careful analysis of how these power imbalances play out between wealthy, well-connected banks and bankers and government enforcement agencies, see Jesse Eisinger, "Why Only One Top Banker Went to Jail for the Financial Crisis," *New York Times Magazine*, Apr. 30, 2014.

wealthiest people in the United States: Wall Street bankers and the profits they made over the course of the early 2000s, before, during, and after the 2008 financial crisis (considered the worst financial crisis since the 1930s Great Depression). Analysts blame the financial crisis on a combination of overly lax mortgage regulations, which allowed (and even encouraged) individuals to acquire unsustainable debts (later called "sub-prime mortgages"), and overly zealous investment bankers, who "falsely assur[ed] investors that securities…were backed by sound mortgages," even though these bankers knew the securities were "full of mortgages that were likely to fail."[69] Ultimately, both the Department of Justice and the Securities and Exchange Commission (the federal agency charged with regulating financial markets) prosecuted investment banks, like Goldman Sachs, along with individual bankers and analysts, like Ralph Cioffi, who knowingly inflated the values of big packages of multiple high-risk (or sub-prime) mortgages.

In nearly every one of these white collar criminal cases, the banking institutions and the individual bankers chose to resolve the charges of securities fraud for sums of money that would be unimaginable to the Ferguson Police Department, let alone to the citizens of Ferguson, or the holders of those individual sub-prime mortgages. For instance, in 2016, Goldman Sachs agreed to pay more than $5 billion in fines and restitution, and Ralph Cioffi agreed to personally pay nearly $1 million in fines—one-third of what the Ferguson Police Department collected in fines and fees in 2015.[70] Though these sums of money are large in the abstract, they are hardly significant to the payors. Goldman Sachs's net annual income is in the trillions, and Ralph Cioffi's salary as a fund manager during the early 2000s was in the millions per year.[71] Cioffi owned multi-million dollar

---

[69] For an example of one of a number of these DOJ financial fraud investigations, see Office of Public Affairs, U.S. Department of Justice, "Goldman Sachs Agrees to Pay More than $5 Billion in Connection with Its Sale of Residential Mortgage Backed Securities," Apr. 11, 2016, https://www.justice.gov/opa/pr/goldman-sachs-agrees-pay-more-5-billion -connection-its-sale-residential-mortgage-backed.

[70] Ibid.; U.S. Securities and Exchange Commission, *SEC v. Ralph R. Cioffi and Matthew M. Tannin*, Civil Action No. 08 2457 (FB) (E.D.N.Y.), "Court Approves SEC Settlements with Two Former Bear Stearns Hedge Fund Portfolio Managers; SEC Bars Managers from Regulated Industries," Litigation Release No. 22398, June 25, 2012, https://www .sec.gov/litigation/litreleases/2012/lr22398.htm.

[71] MarketWatch, "Goldman Sachs Group, Inc.," http://www.marketwatch.com/investing/ stock/gs/financials; William D. Cohan, "Inside the Bear Stearns Boiler Room," *Fortune*,

homes in Manhattan, Long Island, New Jersey, Florida, and Vermont, as well as two Ferrari sports cars.[72] Selling these two cars, alone, would have been sufficient to pay off the fines he was assessed.

Monetary sanctions are just one kind of collateral consequence differentially affecting communities, depending on both race and class demographics. Sex offender regulations, like monetary sanctions, are also subject to the effects of white advantage. For instance, when white Stanford University athlete Brock Turner was found guilty of sexually assaulting an unconscious classmate, a judge sentenced him to only six months in jail—to the frustration of many anti-rape advocates and public defenders, who regularly see less-educated, darker-skinned defendants get longer sentences for lesser crimes.[73] Still, although he served only a brief stint in jail, Turner, like most sex offenders across the United States, will have to register with a publicly accessible database as a sex offender, for the rest of his life.[74]

Turner is lucky to have parents willing to house him in his hometown of Bellbrook, Ohio. The vast majority of sex offenders are neither so privileged in the sentences they receive, nor in their post-incarceration housing choices. In most municipalities and states, people who have been convicted of sex offenses are subject to rigid restrictions on where they can live: not within a mile (or more) of a school, playground, daycare center, or anywhere children gather. In many jurisdictions, the circles of protection around children's institutions overlap, leaving few blocks where those previously convicted of sex offenses can walk, let alone live. In Miami, for instance, locals convicted of sex offenses have found the only location they are legally

Mar. 4, 2009, http://archive.fortune.com/2009/03/02/magazines/fortune/cohan_house-ofcards_full.fortune/index.htm?postversion=2009030306.

[72] Cohan, "Inside the Bear Stearns Boiler Room."

[73] For a public defender's critique of Turner's sentence, see Marcos Barbery, "Op-Ed: Brock Turner's Sentence Proves Again the Advantage of Being White, Well-Off And Educated," Los Angeles Times, Jun. 12, 2016, http://www.latimes.com/opinion/op-ed/la-oe-bar bery-stanford-rape-sentence-20160612-snap-story.html. For a discussion of how the case represents a complex interaction between white privilege and male privilege, see Joseph Margulies, "Race, Class, Feminism . . . and Brock Turner," Newsweek, Sept. 11, 2016, http://www.newsweek.com/race-class-feminism-and-brock-turner-496975.

[74] Amy B. Wang, "Brock Turner Is Now Registered as a Sex Offender in Ohio after Spending Three Months in Jail," Washington Post, Sept. 6, 2016, https://www.washingtonpost.com/news/post-nation/wp/2016/09/06/brock-turner-is-now-registered-as-a-sex-offender-in-ohio-after-spending-three-months-in-jail/?utm_term=.55597ce77075.

permitted to live is in tents under a causeway bridge. Probation officers, supervising clients just released from prison, sometimes take people directly to the bridge, letting them know it is their only housing option.[75]

These policies are particularly irrational in light of what social scientists know about sex offenders. First, their recidivism rates are among the lowest in any category of criminal offense: five percent or lower. (By contrast, the National Institute of Justice estimates that, on average, 68 percent of people convicted of crimes re-offend within three years.)[76] Second, treatment for sex offenders is fairly effective, especially when they maintain community ties. Third, laws designed to keep strangers away from areas where children congregate are unlikely to be especially effective, because only seven percent of sex offenses involve strangers. Moreover, the most serious of these offenders—rapists or serial child abusers—are usually serving the longest prison sentences, and are the least likely to ever be released from prison. The sex offenders registered in community databases and subject to rigid residency restrictions, then, include a wide range of people, many of whom committed less serious crimes than rape or molestation. The definition of "sex offense" and "sex offender" varies by jurisdiction, but can include people convicted of: accessing child pornography online, having sex with a minor (even as a minor), indecent exposure, and urinating in public.[77]

There is little legal justification or sociological evidence, then, for isolating those dozens of sex offenders under that bridge in Miami from their families and communities, preventing them from becoming functioning (and tax-paying) members of society.[78] For now, however, the

[75] Greg Allen, "Sex Offenders Forced to Live Under Miami Bridge," *All Things Considered*, NPR, May 20, 2009, http://www.npr.org/templates/story/story.php?storyId=104150499. For a fictionalized but historically accurate account of life under the Miami Bridge, see Russell Banks, *Lost Memory of Skin* (New York: Ecco, 2011).

[76] Patrick A. Langan, Erica Leah Schmitt, and Matthew R. Durose, *Recidivism Of Sex Offenders Released From Prison In 1994*, NCJ 198281 (Washington, D.C.: Bureau of Justice Statistics, Nov. 16, 2003), https://www.bjs.gov/index.cfm?ty=pbdetail&iid=1136; see also National Institute of Justice, "Recidivism," https://www.nij.gov/topics/corrections/recidivism/Pages/welcome.aspx.

[77] In some jurisdictions, a sixteen year-old can be charged with a sex offense for having sexual relations with another sixteen year-old—on the theory that the participants are too young to freely consent. See generally, Leon, *Sex Fiends*.

[78] This exemplifies the cycle of neoliberal prison reform Story describes in "Prison in the City" as being the dark side of the concept of the million dollar block: sex offender

Miami bridge is just one more example of a collateral consequence, with concentrated and potentially significant community costs.

INSTITUTIONAL COLLATERAL: ILLEGITIMACY

The DOJ report about the "pattern and practice" of police abuses in Ferguson, Missouri hinted at yet another collateral consequence of collateral consequences: institutional and structural disruptions, like the growing community mistrust of police and courts. Such distrust undermines not only community stability, but also trust in law.

Sociologist Katherine Beckett and political scientist Naomi Murakawa have explained the mechanism of this delegitimization as "net widening" through the creation of a "shadow carceral state." They explain that the administrative nature of collateral consequences—like fees associated with incarceration (as in the case of Maria Rivera and her son), arrests associated with fines (as in Ferguson), requirements that those convicted of drug crimes be deported (as in the case of Howard Dean Bailey), or compelling those convicted of sex offenses to live under a bridge (as in Miami)—expand the power of the state over individuals, without expanding the rights of individuals to resist this power.[79] Specifically, Beckett and Murakawa note that expansions in collateral consequences "annex" a whole range of government agencies—from the county clerk's office that collects fines to immigration and family courts—into the criminal justice system. This expands the number of government agencies with the ability to punish individual citizens (or even to undermine citizenship, as in the case of immigration court judges ordering deportations), but provides none of the legal protections that citizens facing punishment in criminal courts typically have.[80] For instance, before a person is sentenced to prison, he or she has a right to a hearing before a judge or a jury,

registration policies like Florida's concentrate and re-concentrate risk in marginalized neighborhoods, and this concentration of risk justifies further surveillance and state intervention.

[79] Katherine Beckett and Naomi Murakawa, "Mapping the Shadow Carceral State: Toward an Institutionally Capacious Approach to Punishment," *Theoretical Criminology* 16, no. 2 (2012): 221–44.

[80] Beckett and Murakawa, "Mapping the Shadow Carceral State," 222.

the right to representation by a lawyer, and the right to confront witnesses against him or her. No such rights attach before collateral consequences are imposed.

Not only do collateral consequences represent expanded state power without comparable expansions in individual rights, but these consequences are, by their nature, less visible than punishments like incarceration. The difficulty the American Bar Association had in identifying and cataloguing these consequences is just one example of their invisibility. The fact that someone like Bailey did not know about the potential collateral consequence of deportation when he pled guilty to a drug charge—and that his lawyer also did not know about these consequences—is another example of invisibility. Hence the term *shadow* carceral state: the network of collateral consequences existing in the United States today is a barely visible projection of the existing criminal justice system, yet, as a "shadow," is taller and wider than the object that casts it.

Scholars have further argued that this shadow carceral state not only has the potential to produce mistrust, delegitimize the government, and expand the power of the government over individual citizens, creating power imbalances, but that it also produces new criminal categories of people.[81] The deported, the sex offender, even the bankrupt mom, or the incarcerated debtor, are stripped of rights and excluded from society, producing new (and newly permanent) groups of stigmatized people, unable to reintegrate into society. Political scientists Amy Lerman and Vesla Weaver have argued that these expanding categories of second-class citizens undermine core democratic values, which now seem only to attach to some people, in some cases.[82] The political exclusions imposed on those with criminal records, as discussed in the next chapter, further exacerbate the challenges individuals with records face in attempting to reintegrate in society.

[81] See Alexa Koenig and Keramet Reiter, "Introduction," in *Extreme Punishment*, Keramet Reiter and Alexa Koenig, eds. (New York: Palgrave Press, 2015); Susan Coutin, "Contesting Criminality: Illegal Migration and Spacialization of Illegality," *Theoretical Criminology* 9, no. 1 (2005): 5–33.

[82] See Amy E. Lerman and Vesla M. Weaver, *Arresting Citizenship: The Democratic Consequences of American Crime Control* (Chicago: University of Chicago Press, 2014).

[4]

THE SILENCED MAJORITY: VOTING RIGHTS AND PRISON-BASED GERRYMANDERING

Eileen Janis grew up on an Indian reservation, as such lands are still legally designated, in South Dakota. She first registered to vote in 1984. Voting was a family tradition for her; Janis's mom taught her to vote, and Janis looked forward to teaching her own son to vote. In November 2008, when her son turned eighteen, she proudly took him to the polls for the first time. They had planned to vote together, carrying on the family tradition. But when Janis arrived at Billie Mills Hall on the Pine Ridge Reservation, and gave her name to poll worker Kyle Clifford, he could not find her name on the voter roll.

Janis insisted that she was registered to vote. She had been registered to vote for nearly a quarter of a century. Clifford called the county auditor's office. Janis stood by. Clifford hung up the phone and informed Janis that her name had been removed from the rolls based on a felony conviction from January of that year. This was the first time Janis learned of her *disenfranchisement*. She had received no notice of the action. Janis was embarrassed, frustrated, and, above all, still determined to vote.

Whereas Chapter Three focused primarily on the social and economic consequences of a criminal conviction, this chapter focuses on the political consequences, specifically voting rights. This chapter begins with Eileen Janis's attempts to reinstate her right to vote, and analyzes how her removal from the South Dakota voter rolls is part of a systematic practice of disenfranchising people—especially minorities—with criminal records across the United States. The chapter next describes the history of felony disenfranchisement, which is one specific characteristic of *civil death* (civiliter mortuus) in the United States, and links disenfranchisement to the history of U.S. slavery. Subsequent sections explore the scope of voting limitations in the United States for both prisoners and former prisoners.

The final section of the chapter examines the impacts of disenfranchisement on electoral districts, voting power, and political outcomes. As it turns out, some towns, especially rural ones, have large populations of prisoners, who are counted in the town census. These non voting prisoners functionally act as bodies that inflate the apparent population of the district, thereby affecting, say, the apportioning of Congressional districts. This practice uncannily resembles the "three-fifths compromise" in the early American republic: the bodies of Southern slaves counted as only three-fifth members of the population, for purposes of census-based allocations of votes and elected representatives. But only nonslaves could vote.

Through an exploration of the invisibilities and silences created by disenfranchisement policies, this chapter explores the implications of who can vote where and asks whether giving prisoners the right to vote would be more democratic (or not).

EILEEN JANIS

As Janis argued with South Dakota poll worker Kyle Clifford about whether she would be allowed to vote, lines of people formed around her. Janis was embarrassed that they had heard about her felony conviction. But she knew her rights. Although she had been convicted of a felony, she had only been sentenced to probation, and probationers are eligible to vote under South Dakota law. Janis insisted that she be permitted to vote. Another poll worker called the auditor's office a second time, confirmed Janis's felony status, and refused to let Janis vote—refused to even let her cast a provisional ballot. Janis left the polls, ashamed.

Still, she knew her rights. So she turned to the local American Civil Liberties Union (ACLU) for help enforcing those rights. As it turned out, another felony probationer, Kim Colhoff, had also been removed from the voting rolls that same year, and her case also came to the attention of the local ACLU. The ACLU filed a lawsuit in federal district court to enforce Janis's and Colhoff's rights to vote, arguing that South Dakota officials had violated state law, improperly removing the names of probationers from the voting rolls. But this was not all.

According to the lawsuit the ACLU filed, the improper removal of Janis and Colhoff from the rolls violated federal law, too. First, the policy had a disproportionate impact on Native Americans, because they were more likely to have felony convictions than whites in South Dakota. In other words, the policy amounted to unconstitutional discrimination, violating the Fourteenth Amendment guarantee of equal protection under the law, regardless of race or background. Second, because Janis and Colhoff never received notice of their removal from the voting polls, the action also violated the Fourteenth Amendment guarantee of due process, which requires that people like Janis and Colhoff get notice of a decision to remove their rights *and* have the opportunity to challenge that decision in court before a judge.[1]

In under a year, South Dakota election officials settled the case. They agreed to pay at least some of the legal fees Janis and Colhoff incurred, and they promised to provide notice and training to state auditors, clarifying the rules about which felons were disqualified from voting under the state constitution. Janis's and Colhoff's voting rights were restored.[2]

Janis was lucky. Under the corrected policy, she was permitted to vote, because she had never served time in prison. Her removal from the voter rolls was a mistake under South Dakota law. Had Janis served time in prison, however, South Dakota would have prohibited her from voting until she finished any parole or probation terms and also took the additional step of re-registering to vote.

[1] *Janis v. Nelson*, First Amended Complaint for Declaratory Relief, Civil Action No. 09-5019 (W.D. S.D. Oct. 7, 2009), https://www.aclu.org/sites/default/files/field_document/2009-10-7-JanisvNelson-FirstAmendedComplaint.pdf.

[2] *Janis v. Nelson*, Settlement Agreement and Release in Full of All Claims, Civil Action No. 09-5019 (W.D. S.D., May 25, 2010), https://www.aclu.org/legal-document/janis-v-nelson-settlement-agreement.

Across the United States, millions of people with felony convictions are prohibited from voting under laws similar to South Dakota's.[3] An untold number of these people might be prohibited from voting, like Janis was, because of mistaken interpretations or overbroad applications of disenfranchisement laws. These laws operate to exclude entire categories of people from voting, like those formerly convicted of felonies. These exclusions, in turn, often have a significantly racially disproportionate impact on certain groups of people, like African-Americans and Native Americans. As it turned out, in spite of the ACLU's advocacy, Janis would have trouble shaking her categorization as one of these excludable citizens.

Two years after South Dakota election officials reinstated Janis on the voter rolls, she again lost her right to vote, but not because of any action she took. In 2012, South Dakota passed a new law: HB1247. The law removed the vote from convicted felons on probation, like Janis, and required her to re-register to vote at the completion of her term of probation.[4] This legal change exemplifies the exceptionally restrictive nature of voting rights for anyone under criminal justice supervision across the United States.

By 2016, 1.6 million people in the United States were in state or federal prison.[5] With the exception of a few thousand prisoners in Maine and Vermont, these 1.6 million prisoners are disenfranchised. They have no right to vote. But this 1.6 million is small in comparison to the 6.1 million—roughly one in every fifty American citizens—who are disenfranchised, but not because they are currently incarcerated. The 6 million

[3] Christopher Uggen, Ryan Lawson, and Sarah Shannon, *6 Million Lost Voters: State-Level Estimates of Felony Disenfranchisement, 2016* (Washington, D.C.: The Sentencing Project, 2016), http://www.sentencingproject.org/publications/6-million-lost-voters-state-level-estimates-felony-disenfranchisement-2016/.

[4] H.B. 1274 (South Dakota), Mar. 19, 2012, http://felonvoting.procon.org/sourcefiles/south-dakota-hb-1274.pdf.

[5] Over 600,000 more people were in jail, and an additional 4.7 million were on probation or parole. For a graphic analysis of incarcerated prison and jail populations, see Peter Wagner and Bernadette Rabuy, "Mass Incarceration: The Whole Pie, 2016," *Prison Policy Initiative*, Mar. 4, 2016, https://www.prisonpolicy.org/reports/pie2016.html. For an analysis of those under community supervision (parole and probation), see Danielle Kaeble and Thomas P. Bonczar, *Probation and Parole in the United States, 2015* (Washington, D.C.: Bureau of Justice Statistics, 2015 NCJ 250230) https://www.bjs.gov/content/pub/pdf/ppus15.pdf.

non-incarcerated disenfranchised voters in the United States include two categories of people: millions who are disenfranchised under state laws, because they are under some form of criminal justice system supervision (like Janis and Colhoff, who were on probation in South Dakota), and millions more who have "served time," but remain disenfranchised because of a prior felony conviction.[6] In some states, former felons are permanently disenfranchised; in other states, the disenfranchisement is temporary, or requires each individual to file a request for permission to be re-listed on the voter roles.[7]

This disenfranchisement is concentrated in specific regions and among specific groups of people. The highest rates of disenfranchisement are in Southern states, like Florida and Mississippi, where *one in ten* citizens is disenfranchised because of prior felony convictions.[8] The impact on racial minorities is even further concentrated. In Florida, Kentucky, Tennessee, and Virginia, at least *one in every five* African-American citizens is disenfranchised.[9] Preliminary research suggests that Latino citizens are disproportionately likely to be disenfranchised relative to non-Latino citizens, as well.[10]

This kind of demographically concentrated disenfranchisement can alter election outcomes in affected states, distorting electoral vote allocations in rural areas with high populations of nonvoting prisoners and distorting voting outcomes in urban areas with high numbers of

[6] Nicole D. Porter, *Expanding the Vote: State Felony Disenfranchisement Reform, 1997–2008* (Washington, D.C.: The Sentencing Project, Oct. 2010), http://www.sentencingproject.org/ wp-content/uploads/2016/01/Expanding-the-Vote-State-Felony-Disenfranchisement-Reform-1997-2010.pdf; Uggen, et al., *6 Million Lost Voters.*

[7] "State Felon Voting Laws," http://felonvoting.procon.org/view.resource.php?resourceID= 000286.

[8] K.K. Rebecca Lai and Jasmine C. Lee, "Why 10% of Florida Adults Can't Vote: How Felony Convictions Affect Access to the Ballot," *New York Times,* Oct. 10, 2016, https:// www.nytimes.com/interactive/2016/10/06/us/unequal-effect-of-laws-that-block-felons-from-voting.html?_r=0.

[9] See Jean Chung, *Felony Disenfranchisement: A Primer* (Washington, D.C.: The Sentencing Project, May 10, 2016), http://www.sentencingproject.org/publications/felony-disenfranchisement-a-primer/.

[10] Marisa J. Demeo and Steven A. Ochoa, *Diminished Voting Power in the Latino Community: The Impact of Felony Disenfranchisement Laws in Ten Targeted States* (Los Angeles: MALDEF, 2003), https://www.maldef.org/assets/pdf/feb18-latinovotingrightsreport.pdf.

disenfranchised citizens. These distortions exacerbate a long history of race- and class-based disenfranchisement policies. In fact, Pippa Holloway, in her history of felony disenfranchisement, argues that the practice is a kind of "modern day poll tax": a policy created specifically to keep socially disadvantaged people from voting.[11]

DISENFRANCHISEMENT: AN AMERICAN TRADITION

Felony disenfranchisement is one facet of the practice of civil death, which excludes those convicted of crimes from various forms of participation in the legal system, as discussed in Chapter Three. Just as the broader practice of civil death existed even in the earliest democratic civilizations, traceable back to Greek and Roman law, and was incorporated into European constitutions over time, so the practice of felony disenfranchisement has been surprisingly integral to democratic constitutions. Countries across the world have long excluded those convicted of crimes from the voting process.

In the seventeenth century, political philosopher John Locke provided a robust theoretical justification for felony disenfranchisement: if a member of society breaks society's rules, that member should be subsequently excluded from the rule-making process.[12] This idea relates to social contract theory, as developed by Thomas Hobbes, John Locke, and Jean-Jacques Rousseau during the Enlightenment. Even before Locke theorized felony disenfranchisement as vital to the social contract, other political theorists argued that it could serve both deterrent—discouraging future offending—and retributive—exacting revenge for criminal acts—purposes.[13]

---

[11] Pippa Holloway, *Living in Infamy: Felon Disenfranchisement and the History of American Citizenship* (New York: Oxford University Press, 2013), xii.

[12] George Brooks, "Felon Disenfranchisement: Law, History, Policy, and Politics," *Fordham Urban Law Journal* 32, no. 5 (2004): 101–48, 103–4.

[13] Angela Behrens, Christopher Uggen, and Jeff Manza, "Ballot Manipulation and the 'Menace of Negro Domination': Racial Threat and Felon Disenfranchisement in the United States, 1850–2002," *American Journal of Sociology* 109, no. 3 (2003): 559–605, 562.

The disenfranchisement of those convicted of crimes was, subsequently, built into the earliest American laws. The U.S. Constitution, as written in 1787, delegated the decision about who could vote to individual states; by the end of the Civil War, twenty-nine states (of thirty-seven) had adopted constitutions that excluded those convicted of crimes from voting.[14] At first, states excluded only people convicted of a few specific offenses from voting, but over time, states passed blanket voting exclusions, encompassing all kinds of convictions.[15]

Of course, until the twentieth century, state and federal law also prohibited voting by a *majority* of the population, including women, African-Americans, and non-property-owners. In the aftermath of the Civil War, the "Reconstruction Amendments," adopted between 1865 and 1870, greatly expanded the scope of the U.S. population with the right to vote. The Thirteenth Amendment abolished slavery. The Fourteenth Amendment extended rights of citizenship and legal protections to anyone born or naturalized in the United States, incorporating African-Americans into full citizenship status. And the Fifteenth Amendment explicitly extended the right to vote to African-American men, prohibiting race- and slavery-based voter exclusions.[16]

Southern states like Alabama, Georgia, and Virginia resisted the Reconstruction Amendments, imposing a battery of barriers to voting, especially for African-Americans: literacy requirements, poll taxes, grandfather clauses (allowing white voters to circumvent the requirements to which black voters were subjected), and, of course, exclusions based on prior criminal convictions.[17] These exclusions were part of the

---

[14] Brooks, "Felon Disenfranchisement," 103–4.

[15] Behrens et al., "Ballot Manipulation," 563.

[16] For a discussion of the Reconstruction Amendments, see Eric Foner, "The Reconstruction Amendments: Official Documents as Social History," *The Gilder Lehrman Institute of American History*, https://www.gilderlehrman.org/history-by-era/reconstruction/essays/reconstruction-amendments-official-documents-social-history.

[17] For an in-depth discussion of the history and development of these laws in one state, Virginia, see Matt Ford, "The Racist Roots of Virginia's Felon Disenfranchisement," *Atlantic*, Apr. 27, 2016, http://www.theatlantic.com/politics/archive/2016/04/virginia-felon-disenfranchisement/480072/.

system of "Jim Crow" laws designed to ensure that former slaves remained systematically oppressed.[18]

These Jim Crow laws amplified exceptions to full citizenship status already codified in the Thirteenth and Fourteenth Amendments. Under the Thirteenth Amendment's "exclusion" clause, those convicted of crimes remained eligible to be enslaved, through an explicit clause permitting slavery when used for punishment. Under Section Two of the Fourteenth Amendment, those convicted of crimes were also foreclosed from voting, through an explicit clause exempting anyone who engages in "participation in rebellion, or other crime" from constitutional protections. By equating slavery with criminality, these exemptions infused racial bias into the constitutional conceptualization of punishment.[19]

In fact, legal scholars have argued that race has driven both the "initial adoption and unusual persistence of felon voting bans."[20] This is another facet of the argument introduced in Chapter Three that identifies the entire network of collateral consequences laws as a "New Jim Crow" system. In some cases, felon-voting bans disproportionately affect

[18] While the Jim Crow laws were concentrated in the Southern parts of the United States, discrimination against African-Americans and practices excluding them from full citizenship and public life existed throughout the United States, in different forms. For particularly thoughtful analyses of collaborations across regions, racial associations, and across the political spectrum, too, see two recent histories of the federal policies undergirding mass incarceration: Naomi Murakawa, *The First Civil Right: How Liberals Built Modern America* (New York: Oxford University Press, 2014); Elizabeth Hinton, *From the War on Poverty to the War on Crime* (Cambridge: Harvard University Press, 2016).

[19] For an analysis of the subtle ways racial bias is written into constitutional law, see Sora Han, *Letters of the Law: Race and the Fantasy of Colorblindness in American Law* (Stanford: Stanford University Press, 2015). For an acknowledgement by correctional professionals of the interrelationship between slavery and punishment, see Harvey Yoder, "Change In Thirteenth Amendment Urged By American Correctional Association," *Harvspot*, Aug. 16, 2016, http://harvyoder.blogspot.com/2016/08/change-in-thirteenth-amendment-urged-by.html. The article describes how, in 2016, the board of governors and delegates at the American Correctional Association adopted a resolution supporting repeal of the "exclusion clause" in the first section of the Thirteenth Amendment—the clause that allows for slavery as punishment for a crime.

[20] Behrens et al., "Ballot Manipulation, 560 (citing, for example, George Fletcher, "Disenfranchisement as Punishment: Reflections on the Racial Uses of Infamia," *UCLA Law Review* 46 (1999): 1895–1908; Andrew L. Shapiro, "Challenging Criminal Disenfranchisement under the Voting Rights Act: A New Strategy," *Yale Law Journal* 103 (1993): 537–66).

African-Americans, but in other cases, the bans disproportionately affect Native Americans, like Eileen Janis. A recent study published in the *American Journal of Sociology* found that felon-voting bans are generally concentrated in states with "large, nonwhite prison populations."[21] In sum, the continued exclusion, in the twenty-first century, of anyone with a prior criminal conviction—and especially nonwhites—from voting rolls raises the question of whether felony disenfranchisement is simply an excuse to extend and entrench the racist, pro-slavery policies of the nineteenth century.

While some Jim Crow era voting restrictions persist into the twenty-first century, others were swept away in the century following the passage of the Reconstruction Amendments. By 1920, women had fought for and earned the right to vote, in both the United States and Europe.[22] In 1965, the Voting Rights Act finally granted suffrage, or the right to vote, to nearly everyone in the United States—sweeping away the Jim Crow restrictions through which Southern states had resisted enforcement of the Fifteenth Amendment. The Voting Rights Act also federalized questions of who could vote—altering the constitutional framework from 1789 that had delegated voting rights determinations to state lawmakers and state constitutions. Just a few years later, in 1971, the right to vote was extended to teenagers—those eighteen and older, at least.

But prisoners and former prisoners remained excluded from voting. Until the Civil War, the number of states disenfranchising both current and former prisoners increased steadily and in tandem. Beginning in the middle of the nineteenth century, states increased their disenfranchisement laws, focusing especially on those in prison. Between the 1950s and 1960s, there was a steep drop-off in the number of states disenfranchising former prisoners, but disenfranchisement of current prisoners remained stable.[23] As of 2016, only thirty-four states disenfranchised

---

[21] Behrens et al., "Ballot Manipulation," 596.

[22] For a discussion of how women were criminalized during this process, being doubly excluded from the vote as women and as criminals, see Simon R. Gardner, "Bind. Torture. Kill. Vote?" *Los Angeles Review of Books*, Oct. 30, 2016, https://lareviewofbooks .org/article/bind-torture-kill-vote/. See also Jill Lepore, *The Secret History of Wonder Woman* (New York: Vintage Books, 2014).

[23] Behrens et al., "Ballot Manipulation," Fig. 1, 567.

prisoners for some period of time following their incarceration, but nearly all states (forty-eight in total) disenfranchised prisoners during their incarceration.[24] In fact, much of the policy debate in the twenty-first century focuses on whether and when the franchise should be extended to former prisoners. But this debate ignores the question of whether current prisoners should be excluded from voting during their incarceration; this has, effectively, been a non-question over the last hundred-plus years.

VOTING IN AND AFTER PRISON

John Locke might have thought that those in prison had broken their promise to abide by the shared values of society and, therefore, deserved to be prohibited from voting. But Locke also lived in a time when the majority of a democracy's population was excluded from voting: women, children, slaves, non-property-owners. Today, the clear trend, in the United States and abroad, has been towards expanding voting rights for all citizens of a given nation: "universal suffrage" is the status quo.

Yet only two of the fifty U.S. state constitutions allow prisoners to vote: Maine's constitution and Vermont's constitution. Maine and Vermont are the two "whitest" states in the United States.[25] This fact provides support for the argument Angela Behrens and colleagues made in their article in the *American Journal of Sociology*: states with higher populations of white prisoners are less likely to disenfranchise all prisoners. Prisoners in Maine and Vermont eagerly exercise their rights to vote, and describe how it helps them to feel more responsible, more socially engaged, more tied to their communities, and, simply, more human.[26]

One other category of detained citizen also has a right to vote throughout the United States: those detained in jails (as opposed to prisons). Most jail detainees are either awaiting a determination of their guilt or

[24] Uggen, et al., *6 Million Lost Voters*.

[25] Luke Roney, "10 U.S. States Are More Than 90% White," *Newser*, Apr. 11, 2016, http://www.newser.com/story/223330/10-us-states-are-more-than-90-white.html.

[26] Spencer Woodman, "Inside a Prison Where Inmates Can Actually Vote for President," *Fusion*, May 10, 2016, http://fusion.net/story/300578/inside-a-vermont-prison-where-inmates-can-vote-president/.

have been sentenced to less than a year of incarceration, for a misdemeanor rather than a felony. Until they are convicted, and even if they are convicted only of a misdemeanor, jail detainees are eligible to vote. One third of the entire incarcerated population in the United States is held in jails (between 600,000 and 700,000 people on any given day), so this is a significant group of incarcerated people with the right to vote.

However, many jail systems do little to encourage jail detainee voting, and this has been the subject of a number of advocacy and awareness-raising campaigns. The American Civil Liberties Union, for instance, has worked with large local jails, like the network of jails in Los Angeles County, to raise awareness of voting rights among detainees and staff. In some cases, the ACLU has also supported detainee lawsuits, seeking to require prison staff to provide voter registration and ballot materials, as in Hawaii in 2004.[27]

Still, the vast majority of prisoners in the United States remain ineligible to vote. The fact that all but two of the United States disenfranchise currently incarcerated prisoners suggests that extending the franchise to currently incarcerated prisoners remains fairly unimaginable across the United States. But elsewhere in the world, democracies are reconsidering the exclusion of even current prisoners from voting rolls.[28]

In 1999, the South African Constitutional Court, that nation's highest court, ordered prisons there to make arrangements to register prisoners to vote and to facilitate prisoner vote casting, arguing that universal suffrage permitted all citizens to vote, and prisoners remained citizens.[29] In 2002, in *Sauvé v. Canada*, the Canadian Supreme Court "unanimously invalidated blanket disenfranchisement legislation."[30] The Court explained that universal

---

[27] Laleh Ispahani and Tricia Forbes, *Voting While Incarcerated: A Toolkit for Advocates Seeking to Register, and Facilitate Voting by, Eligible People in Jail* (New York: American Civil Liberties Union, 2005), 53, https://www.aclu.org/files/pdfs/votingrights/votingwhileincarc_20051123.pdf.

[28] Reuven Ziegler, "Legal Outlier Again? U.S. Felon Suffrage: Comparative and International Human Rights Perspectives," *Boston University International Law Journal*, 29 (2011): 197–266.

[29] *August v. Electoral Commission*, 1999 (3) SA 1 (CC) at 37–38 para. 42 (S. Afr.).

[30] Reuven, "Legal Outlier Again?" 224 (citing *Sauvé v. Canada* [Chief Electoral Officer], [2002] 3 S.C.R. 519, paras. 20–62 [Can.]).

suffrage replaced prior electoral restrictions that sought to enfranchise only a "decent and responsible citizenry." Excluding prisoners from the franchise, the Court argued, was just another attempt to limit voting to the (often arbitrary) category of "decent and responsible" citizens. Disenfranchisement prioritized punitive measures over democratic principles.[31] In 2005 and 2010, the European Court of Human Rights invalidated blanket restrictions on prisoner voting in the United Kingdom and Austria, respectively. In each case, the court found, much like the Canadian court in the *Sauvé* case, that voting is not a privilege, but a legitimizing foundation of any democracy.[32]

Current and former prisoners in the United States have advocated for the right to vote, arguing, like prisoners in South Africa, Canada, and Europe, that felony disenfranchisement violates democratic principles of universal suffrage, and unjustly intensifies the punishment of incarceration. And they have argued that disenfranchisement is racially motivated, or has a racially disproportionate impact. No U.S. court, however, has completely abolished any state's felony disenfranchisement laws.[33]

For now, the rules in the United States about voting from prison remain simple and rigid: outside of Vermont or Maine, prisoners have no right to vote. The rules about voting in jail are also fairly straightforward, although civil liberties advocates have had to work hard to raise awareness of these rules and enforce detainees' rights to access voter registration and voting materials. The rules in the United States about voting *after* prison, however, are complex, varying from state to state and crime to crime. Former prisoners have difficulty learning their rights, let alone knowing how and when they can register to vote. Former prisoners and their advocates have had difficulties enforcing those rights that do exist, too.

Eileen Janis's South Dakota experience provides just one example of the difficulties people convicted of felonies face both in attempting to learn

[31] Ibid.
[32] *Hirst v. U.K.* (No. 2), App. No. 74025/01, 38 Eur. H.R. Rep. 40 (2004) (Fourth Section Chamber); *Hirst v. U.K.* (No. 2), App. No. 74025/01, 42 Eur. H.R. Rep. 41 (recorded 2006) (Grand Chamber); 173 *Frodl v. Austria*, App. No. 20201/04 (Apr. 8, 2010) (First Section Chamber).
[33] Angela Behrens, "Note: Voting—Not Quite a Fundamental Right? A Look at Legal and Legislative Challenges to Felon Disfranchisement Laws," *University of Minnesota Law Review* 89 (2004): 231–75. See also Gardner, "Bind. Torture."

whether they have a right to vote and in exercising that right. South Dakota is now one of twenty-two states that disenfranchises people not only while they are in prison, but also while they are under some other form of criminal justice system supervision. Of these twenty-two states, four disenfranchise people while they are on *parole* (supervision post-prison), and eighteen disenfranchise people while they are on either parole or, like Janis, on *probation* (supervision instead of prison). In these states, former prisoners, parolees, or probationers sometimes have their right to vote automatically reinstated, but at other times, they have to petition to have the right reinstated. The sheer variety in rules across jurisdictions can be hard for the disenfranchised to navigate, and create disparities in who can vote when and where.

The most extreme examples of disenfranchisement, though, come from those states that disenfranchise people for some period of time beyond when their period of criminal justice system supervision (be that prison, parole, or probation) ends. Twelve states do this. Four of these impose lifetime voting bans on anyone with a felony conviction: Florida, Iowa, Kentucky, and Virginia. A fifth state, Arizona, imposes a lifetime ban on anyone with two felony convictions.[34] Unsurprisingly, three of the states with lifetime felony disenfranchisement policies have three of the highest rates of disenfranchised populations: in Florida, Kentucky, and Virginia, more than 7 percent of each state's adult population is disenfranchised. In Florida alone, more than 1.5 million individuals have been disenfranchised due to felony convictions. As noted earlier, these Southern states also have rates of African-American disenfranchisement as high as one in every four African-Americans.[35]

VOTING RIGHTS AND DISTORTIONS

The relationship between prisoners and voting has distorted American politics in a number of ways. The first way is obvious: millions of people have been banned from voting in local, state, and federal elections. If all

[34] Uggen, et al., *6 Million Lost Voters*; "Editorial: Virginia's Republicans Turn Back the Clock," *New York Times*, Sept. 9, 2016, http://www.nytimes.com/2016/09/10/opinion/virginias-republicans-turn-back-the-clock.html?action=click&pgtype=Homepage&clickSource=story-heading&module=opinion-c-col-left-region&_r=1.

[35] Uggen, et al., *6 Million Lost Voters*.

6 million of these people were permitted to vote, and if they exercised their rights and did vote, these votes could certainly sway election outcomes.

This leads to a second potential distortion related to felony disenfranchisement: politicians have incentives to permit or prohibit people with felonies from voting, depending on what they perceive will be helpful in an election year. For instance, in 2016, Virginia's democratic governor Terry McAuliffe sought to restore the votes of 200,000 disenfranchised prisoners through an executive order. It was April of a presidential election year. McAuliffe said he was motivated by wanting these prisoners "back in society" and "feeling good" about themselves. But might he also have been motivated by a hope that re-enfranchised prisoners would vote in his and his party's favor in November?[36] Perhaps this possibility scared state Republican legislators; they brought litigation challenging the constitutionality of the governor's executive order, arguing he had overstepped his constitutional authority. Virginia's state supreme court agreed with the Republican legislators, and explained that the governor could only restore voting rights case by case. As of early 2017, Governor McAuliffe had reviewed and restored voting rights in 13,000 cases.

In other states, too, politicians, who have sought to reform felon voting bans, have faced debates and pressures similar to those simmering in Virginia. The battles have included contradictory lawmaking between executive orders and legislative initiatives, polarization along party lines, and compromises that result in confusing new regulations allowing some kinds of felons to vote—the nonviolent, those in jail but not prison, or those not involved in crimes of "moral turpitude," however that might be interpreted.[37]

---

[36] Indeed, McAuliffe was an especially well-connected Democrat; former president Bill Clinton picked him to lead the Democratic National Committee in 2000, and he co-chaired Hillary Clinton's 2008 presidential campaign. His own campaign finances, as well as his funding and financial relationships with the Clintons, have been investigated by the media and the FBI alike. Jordan Fabian, "McAuliffe Heads Off Probe That Could Hurt Clinton," *The Hill*, May 28, 2016, http://thehill.com/homenews/campaign/281429-mcauliffe-heads-off-probe-that-could-hurt-clinton.

[37] Uggen, et al., *6 Million Lost Voters*, 12.

The debate over whether to reinstate felon-voting rights often revolves around whether disenfranchisement is socially racist or individually justified. For instance, in a 2016 opinion piece chiding Virginia's Republican lawmakers for resisting felon-voting reforms, the *New York Times* editorial board accused the politicians of seeking "to protect a racist and vindictive practice that should have been consigned to history long ago."[38] Meanwhile, Republicans continued to resist the restoration of felon voting rights, arguing that McAuliffe's move was politically opportunistic in an election year, and that former prisoners must prove themselves worthy of a second chance in some way.[39] Ultimately, in the 2016 presidential election, Donald Trump beat Hillary Clinton by just a few thousand votes in a few key "swing" states (despite losing the popular vote by millions). Journalists speculated that felony disenfranchisement might have functionally determined a major election outcome.[40]

In Florida, which has the dubious reputation of being home to almost one-quarter of all the disenfranchised people in the United States (1.5 of 6.1 million), such arguments received particular attention in an earlier election year: in 2000, when George W. Bush was running against Al Gore in a close presidential campaign. In the end, Bush won Florida by the extraordinarily narrow margin of 537 votes (out of 6 million cast in that state), although a Supreme Court ruling prevented the ballots from being rigorously counted.[41] Thereby granted Florida's electoral votes,

---

[38] "Editorial: Virginia's Republicans."

[39] "Republicans: Virginia Gov. McAuliffe Restored Felon Voting Rights to Help Clinton, 'Political Opportunism,'" *FoxNews.com*, Apr. 23, 2016, http://www.foxnews.com/politics/2016/04/23/republicans-virginia-gov-mcauliffe-restored-felon-voting-rights-to-help-clinton-political-opportunism.html.

[40] For an analysis of the close "swing" states, see James Barrett, "How Many Votes Did Trump & Clinton Get? The Final Vote Count," *The Daily Wire,* Dec. 21, 2016, http://www.dailywire.com/news/11777/how-many-votes-did-trump-and-clinton-get-final-james-barrett. For journalists speculating about the impact of disenfranchisement, see Melissa Franqui, "Felony Disenfranchisement: The Untold Story of the 2016 Election," *Salon,* Nov. 28, 2016, http://www.salon.com/2016/11/28/felony-disenfranchisement-the-untold-story-of-the-2016-election_partner/; Kamala Kelkar, "This Year, Laws with Roots to the Civil War Prevented 6.1 Mllion from Voting," *PBS NewsHour,* Nov. 13, 2016, http://www.pbs.org/newshour/updates/civil-war-laws-prevented-voting/.

[41] *Bush v. Gore*, 531 U.S. 98 (2000).

Bush collected enough electoral votes to win the presidency.[42] But had even 10 percent of the disenfranchised citizens in Florida been able to vote, and had they been even marginally in favor of either the Republican or the Democratic candidate, their votes easily could have changed the outcome of the election in one state, and therefore in the nation.

Many "maybes" and "ifs" plague this argument about the role of felony disenfranchisement in the 2000 and 2016 elections: would re-enfranchised former felons have actually voted, and, if so, how would they have voted? Dozens of analyses later, many scholars and politicians have argued that re-enfranchising former felons in Florida would have likely favored the Democratic candidate, Al Gore. These arguments are based on an analysis of which voters were "purged" from Florida's voter rolls in 2000. Prior to the election, the Republican secretary of state (serving under George W. Bush's brother, then-Governor Jeb Bush), Katherine Harris, who was also co-chairwoman of Bush's presidential campaign in Florida, oversaw the purging of the voter rolls in the state, in an attempt to ensure that everyone voting was properly registered to vote. Foreshadowing Eileen Janis's incorrect purging from the voter rolls in South Dakota in 2008, later reviews of the Florida purge revealed that as many as 12,000 voters were erroneously purged from Florida's voting rolls. Of the purged voters, 44 percent were African-American. This means the percentage of black voters purged from the rolls was more than four times greater than the percentage of black residents in Florida (10 percent). And African-Americans overwhelmingly vote for Democratic candidates in major U.S. elections. Even those 12,000 erroneously purged voters could easily have changed the election outcome in 2000.[43]

Felon voter disenfranchisement, and the associated purging (whether accurate or inaccurate) of voter rolls, is just one way that current and former prisoner populations can potentially distort the voting process. Another way current prisoners, in particular, distort the voting process is by being counted as residents in voting districts where they have no right

---

[42] Holloway, *Living in Infamy*, xii.

[43] Holloway, *Living in Infamy*, xii; Myrna Peréz, *Voter Purges* (New York: Brennan Center for Justice, 2008), 3, https://www.brennancenter.org/sites/default/files/legacy/public ations/Voter.Purges.f.pdf.

to vote. This (mis)counting makes these districts look more populous than they actually are, distorting the representativeness of both the districts and the voters, or the principle of "one person, one vote." Specifically, the 1.6 million people in prison in the United States distort census counts in the (primarily rural) areas where they are imprisoned, affecting the way voting district lines are drawn. Most people convicted of crimes lived in major urban areas at the time of their crime. But most serve their time in rural counties, hundreds of miles from those urban centers.[44] These urban, prisoner transplants count, for census purposes, as residents of the rural prison towns in which they live. These towns, in turn, look like they have a larger voting population than they actually do, so they are allocated more representatives.[45] In essence, rural prison towns get more votes than their voting population warrants.

Examples of this phenomenon are easy to find. For instance, in Illinois, 60 percent of all the prisoners in the state were residing in Cook County, which includes Chicago, before they were incarcerated. Of the 50,000 people in prison in Illinois, then, 30,000 are from Chicago and the immediately surrounding areas. But nearly all of these Chicagoans are incarcerated outside of Cook County and, therefore, counted in other counties' census statistics for purposes of drawing voting districts. Likewise, in Texas, 12 percent of the population in one rural voting district is incarcerated. One in eight "residents" of that rural district, in other words, cannot vote, yet these nonvoting residents are still counted in local census statistics, used in drawing voting districts. This means eighty-eight voting residents in the rural Texas district are represented as if they are one hundred residents from an urban area, like Houston or Dallas. Conversely, each resident of the rural Texas district has a vote that counts like the vote of around 1.1 people. This *prison-based gerrymandering* does not just

[44] See *The Justice Atlas of Sentencing and Corrections* for an interactive map visually displaying these facts: http://www.justiceatlas.org/; Ruth Wilson Gilmore, *Golden Gulag: Prisons, Surplus, Crisis, and Opposition in Globalizing California* (Berkeley: University of California Press, 2007).

[45] Peter Wagner, Aleks Kajstura, Elena Lavarreda, Christian de Ocejo, and Sheila Vennell O'Rourke, "Fixing Prison-Based Gerrymandering after the 2010 Census: A 50 State Guide" (Northampton Prison Policy Initiative, 2010). Interactive map available online at: http://www.prisonersofthecensus.org/50states/.

inflate the votes of people residing in districts with prisons, or reduce the voting population elsewhere; it also deflates the votes of people residing in districts without prisons.[46]

Felony disenfranchisement often eludes detection. At the moment a person pleads guilty to a felony, he or she acquires the status of felon and loses a range of rights usually attaching to citizenship, including, in most states, the right to vote. At that moment of the guilty plea, no judge is required to tell a felon about the loss of the right to vote. And many former felons do not learn of this loss until, like Eileen Janis at the polls in 2008, they attempt to exercise the right they thought they had. Even once Janis became aware of the loss of her right, though, she had little way of knowing how many others had shared her experience. Finding out required class action litigation; concerted, county-by-county and state-by-state social science research; and years of analysis.

And even with all this litigation and research, the impact of stripping millions of Eileen Janises of their rights to vote remains largely unknown. Would her vote have changed her local election outcome in 2008? Would the votes of those thousands of disenfranchised felons in Virginia have changed the election outcomes in 2016, and would the votes of those 1.5 million disenfranchised felons in Florida have changed the election outcome in 2000? We can make educated guesses, but we can never know for sure. What we *do* know is that the simple act of stripping felons (and former felons) of the right to vote—a policy that dates back to the earliest democracies—turns out to have ripple effects on individuals, communities, and even entire political systems.

---

[46] *The Prison Gerrymandering Project*, Prison Policy Initiative, http://www.prisonersof thecensus.org/impact.html. Visit this website to explore the impacts of prison gerry mandering state-by-state and county-by-county. Note, of course, that prisoners are not housed in rural areas for the purpose of distorting voter demographics and districts. Prison siting is a complicated process often involving political and economic negotiations, as discussed briefly in Chapter Five, in the discussion of the relationship between private prisons and prison siting decisions.

[5]

PRISONS FOR PROFIT: PRIVATIZATION AND THE PRISON INDUSTRIAL COMPLEX

The unusual name "Hutto" crops up in surprising places in the history of mass incarceration. Hutto is the name of the petitioner in a 1978 U.S. Supreme Court case: *Hutto v. Finney.* In this case, the Supreme Court upheld a broad application of the Eighth Amendment prohibition against cruel and unusual punishment to prison conditions across Arkansas. T. Don Hutto is also the name of an immigration detention facility in Taylor, Texas, 160 miles west of Houston, opened in 2006. And Terrell Don Hutto is the cofounder and a current member of the board of directors of the Corrections Corporation of America, (now CoreCivic), a publicly traded company reporting an annual revenue of $1.7 billion. Terrell Hutto has worked in Texas, Arkansas, Virginia, and Tennessee over a career spanning more than fifty years. Tracing the Hutto name through court cases, detention centers, and private financial documents across the American South reveals the mechanisms by which prison privatization gained popularity across the United States in the late twentieth and early twenty-first centuries.

Fewer than 10 percent of all U.S. prisoners are housed in private prison facilities. So the American prison system can hardly be called "privatized." But even in the vast majority of prisons and jails still publicly operated by federal, state, and local governments, private corporations have a stake in providing the enormous resources—such as food, medical care, and utilities like electricity, water, and phone service—required to run any self-contained institution. In most prisons, private corporations provide at least some of these resources and services, make a profit from these provisions, and thereby become invested in maintaining a large prison system.

Although American prisons are not wholly privatized, imprisonment in America has become an industry, complete with investors, publicly traded stocks, political lobbyists, and public relations experts.

This chapter first explores the relationship between mass incarceration and the partial privatization of U.S. prisons, as exemplified by the career of one pivotal figure in this history: Terrell Don Hutto. The chapter then examines the relationship between profit motives and justice motives, tracing the costs and benefits of prison privatization, and analyzing the measurement and interpretation challenges that have plagued attempts to assess the impacts of privatization. In particular, two policy analyses of two attempts by national agencies to limit and constrain privatization—one by the Department of Justice and one by the Federal Communications Commission—highlight the robust debates about the costs and benefits of privatizing punishment.

Through these narratives of business building and reform, this chapter examines the many players in the prison industry, identifying the often-surprising groups of "payers" (e.g., prisoners and family members of prisoners) and "profiteers" (e.g., private corporations and politicians negotiating contracts with them) from America's massive investment in incarceration. Some argue that even partial privatization is both efficient and transparent, while others argue that privatization promotes opacity, and inefficiency, and also incentivizes injustice. This chapter investigates these controversies, and examines whether profitability and justice can ever harmoniously coexist.

T. DON HUTTO AND THE BIRTH
OF THE PRIVATE PRISON

For the first twenty-or-so years of his career, Hutto was something of a humane reformer. Terrell Don Hutto was born in 1935 in Sinton, Texas. He was a schoolteacher, who eventually found his way into working in prison, as an educator in the Texas Department of Criminal Justice in the 1960s.[1] He soon moved up the ranks of prison officials to become assistant

---

[1] James Estrin, "Showcase: A Wide View of a Hellish World," *New York Times*, May 27, 2009, http://lens.blogs.nytimes.com/2009/05/27/showcase-a-wide-view-of-a-hellish-world/;

warden, and then warden, of a prison in Huntsville, Texas. By 1971, Hutto was a "nationally-respected, reform-minded administrator."[2]

Meanwhile, in Hutto's neighboring state of Arkansas, the prison system was facing increasing scrutiny from a federal judge named Jesse Smith Henley. The state's legal troubles started in 1965, when three prisoners housed in the Arkansas State Penitentiary filed a lawsuit describing the horrific treatment they regularly experienced: electric shocks, punitive rape, and forced labor. The Tucker Unit, one of the prison farms making up the state penitentiary, even bequeathed its name to a torture device: the "Tucker" telephone, a machine with two electrocuted wires, which could be attached to a misbehaving prisoner's big toe and penis, and used to shock him.

Judge Henley described being sent to prison in Arkansas as "a banishment from civilized society to a dark and evil world completely alien to the free world."[3] The Supreme Court would later note, matter-of-factly: "That characterization was amply supported by the evidence."[4] Although Arkansas prisoners initially complained about conditions in just one prison, Judge Henley was disturbed by the conditions throughout the state prison system, and soon was overseeing reforms in multiple prisons. The lawsuit in Arkansas, and the state's reform efforts, made national news, and quickly became politically polarizing.

Robert Sarver, the state's Commissioner of Corrections, supported the reforms, but his relations with the state legislature frayed as he demanded more and more money to support a better prison system.[5] By 1971, Arkansas Governor Dale Bumpers was looking around for someone to

Ellis Widner, "Photos of Cummins: A Window into Arkansas History," *Arkansas Online*, May 17, 2009, http://www.arkansasonline.com/news/2009/may/17/photos-cummins-window-arkansas-history/.

[2] Malcolm M. Feeley and Edward L. Rubin, *Judicial Policy Making and the Modern State: How the Courts Reformed America's Prisons* (New York: Cambridge University Press, 1998): 66.

[3] "Arkansas Prison System Undergoing Massive Reform," *Reading Eagle*, Feb. 10, 1972: 11, https://news.google.com/newspapers?nid=1955&dat=19720210&id=iQcrAAAAIBAJ&sjid=Y5gFAAAAIBAJ&pg=4418,5631048.

[4] *Hutto v. Finney*, 437 U.S. 678, 682 (1978).

[5] See "Arkansas Prison System."

replace Sarver. The perfect candidate turned out to be right next door in Texas: then-warden Terrell Don Hutto.

Hutto took over the Arkansas system and managed it throughout the 1970s. He would navigate judicial scrutiny, media scandals, and ongoing reform pressures. In spite of Hutto's reformist background, however, abuses—and litigation—continued in Arkansas throughout his tenure.

Even nonprisoners experienced the abuse. In December 1971, not long after Hutto took over the Arkansas prisons, Willie Stewart, a seventeen-year-old, 112-pound boy visited the Cummins Unit at the Arkansas State Penitentiary for the day as part of the "one-day wonders" program. Stewart was a "first-time offender," and the program was designed to expose at-risk youth to the unpleasantness of prison, in order to discourage them from further illegal behavior.[6] "One-day wonders" was a precursor of "scared straight" programs, which had similar ends, albeit usually with gentler means. By the early 2000s, systematic evaluations of such programs found that they were often associated with *higher* crime rates for participants than nonparticipants, and tended to be more harmful than doing nothing at all.[7] As it turned out, though, Willie Stewart would never have the opportunity to do anything illegal again.

When he arrived at the Cummins Unit, Stewart was chased, shot at, dunked in water, forced to do push-ups, and then to pick cotton, until he collapsed. Seventeen-year-old Willie Stewart died on the way to the hospital. At the time Stewart died, Commissioner Hutto had already received numerous complaints about the "one-day wonders" program, but he had apparently not investigated it. One-day wonders was, in fact, part of Arkansas' prison reform efforts. The program continued following Stewart's death.[8]

---

[6] Nicholas C. Chriss, "Cummins Prison Farm Source of Controversy Again," *Tuscaloosa News*, Dec. 19, 1971: 16E, https://news.google.com/newspapers?nid=1817&dat=19711219&id=7f0cAAAAIBAJ&sjid=IJwEAAAAIBAJ&pg=7435,4831508.

[7] Anthony Petrosino, Carolyn Turpin Petrosino, and John Buehler, *"Scared Straight" and Other Juvenile Awareness Programs for Preventing Juvenile Delinquency,* Campbell Systematic Reviews, May 2002, updated June 2011, https://www.campbellcollaboration.org/media/k2/attachments/Petrosino_Scared_Straight_Update.pdf; Lawrence W. Sherman, Denise Gottfredson, Doris MacKenzie, John Eck, Peter Reuter, and Shawn Bushway, *Preventing Crime: What Works, What Doesn't, What's Promising,* A Report to the United States Congress, prepared for the National Institute of Justice, 1997, https://www.ncjrs.gov/works/.

[8] See Chriss, "Cummins Prison Farm."

Hutto's early challenges in Arkansas undoubtedly shaped his later career choices in the private prison sector—where he would lead corporations in systematically avoiding public scrutiny, successfully navigating abuse scandals, and occasionally propagating policies that turned out to do more harm than good. But first, Hutto would put in a few more years in the public sector, this time in Virginia.

By the time the Supreme Court weighed in on the unconstitutional conditions of confinement throughout the Arkansas prisons, in the case of *Hutto v. Finney* in 1978, Terrell Don Hutto had moved on to become the Director of Corrections in Virginia. There, he took over a prison system facing a different challenge: increasingly severe overcrowding. In 1979, the average sentence to prison in Virginia was two and one-half years, earning Virginia a place among the top ten states with the longest prison sentences—even though such a sentence seems short by twenty-first century standards. Hutto was adamant that Virginia needed to relinquish its top-ten position by shortening average prison sentences.

In the late 1970s and early 1980s, Hutto's name appeared regularly in the *Washington Post*, as he warned of soaring costs and endless litigation if Virginia did not commit to significant criminal justice system reforms, such as shorter prison sentences, increased use of probation and parole instead of prison, and unpaid community service programs as an additional alternative to prison.[9] Virginia, like the rest of the United States, was at a turning point: would the state roll back prison sentences and implement alternatives to incarceration, or would it build more prisons to comply with court orders requiring better (and more spacious) conditions of confinement?[10]

In retrospect, we know that Virginia, like the country, was perched at the brink of mass incarceration. Virginia ignored Hutto's recommendations, instead building more and more prisons and imposing longer and longer sentences. In 1997, barely twenty years after Hutto first took over Virginia's prison system, the average sentence to prison in Virginia was

[9] J. Regan Kerney, "Va. Prison Report Cites Overcrowding," *Washington Post*, Apr. 17, 1979: C-1.

[10] For an analysis of how another state (Florida) negotiated this process, see Heather Schoenfeld, "Mass Incarceration and the Paradox of Prison Conditions Litigation," *Law and Society Review* 44 (2010): 732–68.

close to nine years—almost four times longer than the average had been in 1979 (but only just above the 1997 nationwide average).[11]

At some point, Hutto must have realized that his recommendations were going unheeded—and that mass incarceration would present other career opportunities. In 1982, he resigned "suddenly and unexpectedly" from his position as director of the Virginia Department of Corrections. Local newspapers speculated about why: was it political, personal, a secretive career move? Maybe the newly elected Democratic governor was unsupportive of Hutto's prison reform plans?[12]

As it turned out, Hutto would not stray very far from politics. Just one year after he resigned from his position in Virginia, in 1983, he resurfaced, with yet another "director" title, this time with a new, private entity called Corrections Corporation of America. CCA had a bold business plan: provide private prison beds, quickly and cheaply, to states grappling with overcrowded prisons. Two businessmen, Thomas Beasley and Robert Crants, recruited Hutto to their enterprise for his insider's corrections knowledge. (Beasley had formerly chaired the Tennessee Republican Party.[13]) Hutto brought legitimacy to this new business model and served as a bridge to corrections professionals. In fact, in 1984, he became president of the American Correctional Association, the leading professional association for prison workers and a body that reviews and offers professional accreditation (for a fee) to prisons across the United States.

Although Hutto moved from being a state employee to being the director of a private corporation, and also the president of a professional nonprofit, he remained deeply involved in politics. Hutto's early career, managing lawsuits alleging abuse in prison, grappling with a burgeoning prison population, and advocating politically for more funding for prisons, would turn out to be invaluable in CCA's work. At first, convincing states, or the federal

---

[11] Paul M. Ditton and Doris James Wilson, *Truth in Sentencing in State Prisons* (Washington, D.C.: Bureau of Justice Statistics, Jan. 1999), NCJ 170032: Table 8, http://bjs.gov/content/pub/pdf/tssp.pdf.

[12] "Corrections' Chief's Plans to Quit Surprise Officials," *Free Lance-Star*, Dec. 11, 1981: 17.

[13] Margaret Talbot, "The Lost Children: What Do Tougher Detention Policies Mean for Illegal Immigrant Families?" *New Yorker*, Mar. 3, 2008, http://www.newyorker.com/magazine/2008/03/03/the-lost-children.

government, or labor unions representing prison workers, to cede control of prison facilities to a private corporation was no easy task. Beasley worked connections in his home state of Tennessee, and CCA leadership looked for opportunities where states were facing pressure from federal judges to reduce overcrowding, or where federal agencies were short on beds.

CCA's first contracts came in 1983 and 1984 from Tennessee (Beasley's home state)—for a jail and juvenile detention center—and from the federal government—to design and maintain an immigration detention facility in Texas (Hutto's home state). The contract to take over the Hamilton County jail in Tennessee represented the first time a private corporation had ever had sole responsibility for running a prison or jail. The Texas facility required even more work. The CCA website describes the pragmatism required to get this first private detention facility off the ground: Hutto and Beasley found an old motel to lease for bed space, and Hutto ran to Walmart and used his personal credit card to buy toiletries for the new detainees. Hutto fondly remembers: "At one point they were running to a Houston hardware store for supplies. It was a start-up before start-ups were fashionable. We met the deadline, the detainees arrived, and a new relationship was forged between government and the private sector."[14]

This new relationship would be long-lasting, politicized, and fraught. At first, however, the local Hamilton County government in Tennessee and the federal government signing the Texas detention center contract were hopeful that CCA would run the jails more efficiently than any government agency could, saving taxpayers money. Many other cities, counties, and states shared a similar hope.

PRISONS, PROFITS, AND PROBLEMS

In 1988, after CCA had "gone public," selling shares in the open market on Wall Street, and while their stock price was rising, Beasley described the simplicity of their business model: private corporations do things better than

[14] Damon Hininger, "T. Don Hutto: The Mettle of the Man Behind Our Proud Facility," *Corrections Corporation of America,* Jan. 19, 2010, http://www.cca.com/insidecca/ t.-don-hutto-%E2%80%93-the-mettle-of-the-man-behind-our-proud-facility.

the government. In 1988, the time was right to sell a privatization model; Margaret Thatcher was privatizing public services in the United Kingdom, and U.S. politicians were eager to follow this model.[15] Beasley explained that when he presented the idea of prison privatization, people only resisted briefly: "Their first impulse is to say only the government can do it, because only the government's ever done it. But their second reaction is that the government can't do anything very well." After that, "you just sell it like you were selling cars or real estate or hamburgers." Beasley summed up: "We're the best thing that ever happened to corrections since they stopped beating 'em."[16]

The beatings, however, never did stop, especially not in privately run prison facilities. Investigations and exposés in 1998 in Ohio, 2004 in Maryland, 2008 in Texas, 2010 in Idaho, and 2016 across the United States, all revealed mismanaged prisons, frequent escapes, unnecessary deaths, and vicious beatings. One of these exposés, a 2008 *New Yorker* article, examined the T. Don Hutto Residential Center in Texas, named after none other than the founder of CCA, and run by the same corporation. Hutto's namesake facility had been keeping children in immigration detention with their parents (who were mostly awaiting asylum decisions), but treating the children like criminals: ordering them around, waking them up for counts in the middle of the night, and threatening to permanently separate them from their parents.[17] Each time one of these exposés of a CCA facility or facilities hit the news, CCA stock suffered, but soon recovered.[18]

[15] For an overview of privatization in the United Kingdom under Margaret Thatcher, see Richard Seymour, "A Short History of Privatisation in the UK: 1979–2012," *The Guardian*, Mar. 29, 2012, https://www.theguardian.com/commentisfree/2012/mar/29/short-history-of-privatisation. For an early review about the debates over privatization in the United States, see Ronald C. Moe, "Exploring the Limits of Privatization," *Public Administration Review* 47, no. 6 (Nov./Dec., 1987): 453–60. For an overview of empirical studies of state privatization efforts, see William L. Megginson and Jeffry M. Netter, "From State to Market: A Survey of Empirical Studies on Privatization," *Journal of Economic Literature* 39, no. 2 (June 2001): 321–89.

[16] Erik Larson, "Captive Company," *Inc.*, June 1, 1988, http://www.inc.com/magazine/19880601/803.html.

[17] Talbot, "The Lost Children."

[18] Madison Pauly, "A Brief History of America's Private Prison Industry," *Mother Jones*, Jul./Aug. 2016, http://www.motherjones.com/politics/2016/06/history-of-americas-private-prison-industry-timeline. See also Associated Press, "Idaho: FBI Enters Investigation into Prison Operator," *New York Times*, Mar. 8, 2014: A-12.

While CCA executives tried to limit their investments of time and money in new prison and detention facilities (by minimizing the ratio of prisoners or detainees to staff, providing little training to staff, and permitting few comforts to prisoners or detainees), they were generous in investing time and money in politics. As it turned out, Beasley and Hutto had to do more than sell privatization like hamburgers. They had to develop the infrastructure to ensure privatization continued to be needed, the way it had been needed during the spate of prison overcrowding litigation in the late 1970s and early 1980s, when CCA was first conceived.

In particular, CCA executives became involved with the American Legislative Exchange Counsel (ALEC), co-chairing the Counsel's criminal justice task force in the 1980s, and attending their meetings on immigration policy in the early 2000s. In both cases, ALEC authored and advocated for new legislation to increase criminal sentences and immigration penalties, which in turn contributed to increasing incarceration rates in the 1990s and increasing immigration detention rates in the 2000s.[19] CCA officials have since limited their relationships with ALEC, publicly disassociating themselves in 2010.[20] But, as the American Civil Liberties Union noted in a recent report, CCA officials continue to see any shortening of criminal sentences, or decreased reliance on mass incarceration, as a threat to their business model.[21]

In order to further strengthen the infrastructure of privatization, CCA has worked at the local level, targeting county commissioners and judges. Corporate CCA officials collaborate with these local officials to negotiate contracts and issue bonds to fund the building of new private prison facilities. Often, the agreements to fund these facilities are "on spec,"

[19] Ibid.
[20] Bob Ortega, "Political Ties Give Leverage to CCA," *Arizona Republic*, Sept. 4, 2011.
[21] See David Shapiro, *Banking on Bondage: Private Prisons and Mass Incarceration* (New York: American Civil Liberties Union, Nov. 2011), 18, https://www.aclu.org/files/assets/bankingonbondage_20111102.pdf. The report notes that "As CCA stated in its 2010 Annual Report, under the heading 'Risks Related to Our Business and Industry,' '[l]egislation has been proposed in numerous jurisdictions that could lower minimum sentences for some nonviolent crimes and make more inmates eligible for early release based on good behavior. Also, sentencing alternatives under consideration could put some offenders on probation ... who would otherwise be incarcerated.'"

coordinated with the goal of attracting state or federal agency contracts for extra detainee bed space, but the institutions are built before such contracts are secured. In these deals, CCA seeks financial support from local jurisdictions to expand the company's infrastructure; in turn, the local jurisdictions hope to attract further investments from state and federal agencies, while also creating local jobs. Of course, in some cases, the speculation is only wishful thinking: the prisons remain empty, and the local jurisdictions, not CCA, suffer the cost of the failed investment gamble.[22]

So far, CCA has weathered frequent fluctuations in the demand for private prison beds, and changes to sentencing laws and other correctional infrastructure, with equanimity—and relative success. Over the past thirty years, since CCA took over those first facilities in Texas and Tennessee, they have signed hundreds more contracts to take over jails and prisons across the United States.[23] Today, CCA is a publicly traded, multimillion dollar company. As of 2016, one in every twenty U.S. prisons was privately operated.[24] In total, just over 130,000 people in prison in the United States are in private prisons. This means roughly one in every ten prisoners is in a private prison.[25] Even more immigration detention facilities are privately operated. Nine of the ten largest detention facilities are privately operated, and more than half of all detained immigrants are in private facilities, most of them run either by CCA or its only major competitor, the GEO Group.[26]

[22] Sasha Abramsky, "Incarceration, Inc.," *The Nation*, Jul. 1, 2004, https://www.thenation. com/article/incarceration-inc/. For an extended discussion of the relationship between economics, labor, and prison siting decisions, see Ruth Wilson Gilmore, *Golden Gulag: Prisons, Surplus, Crisis, and Opposition in Globalizing California* (Berkeley: University of California Press, 2007).

[23] Amy Cheung, "Prison Privatization and the Use of Incarceration" (Washington, D.C.: The Sentencing Project, 2002, updated 2004), https://www. prisonlegalnews.org/ media/publications/Prison%20Privatization%20and%20the%20Use%20of%20 Incarceration%2C%20Sentencing%20Project%2C%202000.pdf.

[24] J. J. Stephan. *Census of State and Federal Correctional Facilities*, 2005, NCJ 222182 (Washington, D.C.: U.S. Department of Justice, Bureau of Justice Statistics, Oct. 2010).

[25] Peter Wagner, "Public & Private Prisons, 1999–2014," Prison Policy Institute, http:// www.prisonpolicy.org/graphs/public_vs_private_1999-2014.html.

[26] Bethany Carson and Eleana Diaz, "Payoff: How Congress Ensures Private Prison Profit with an Immigrant Detention Quota," *Grassroots Leadership*, Apr. 2015, http://grassrootsleadership.org/reports/payoff-how-congress-ensures-private-prison -profit-immigrant-detention-quota#3.

ARE PRIVATE PRISONS CHEAPER AND BETTER?

Proponents say private prisons are more efficient than government bureau-cracies: they hold more prisoners at a lower cost per person per day than government-run facilities. Opponents say private prison corporations get unfair tax breaks, with taxation rates as low as 4 to 5 percent—among the lowest of any U.S. corporate taxation rates and about one-quarter of the average U.S. worker's income tax rate.[27] And, opponents say, private prisons cut costs by ignoring basic rights, or by finding creative ways to "cut corners" in provid-ing medical care, training staff, and meeting prisoners' most basic needs.[28]

Proponents say private prisons have incentives to succeed along vari-ous metrics: keeping costs down, keeping prisoners and staff safe, lowering recidivism rates. Opponents say private prisons have incentives to make profits: lobbying for harsher and longer sentences to keep their beds filled, ignoring prisoners' expensive medical needs, minimizing staff training.[29]

Proponents say publicly traded companies like the Corrections Cor-poration of America and the GEO Group must compete to earn govern-ment contracts and adhere to strict financial rules, all of which promotes transparency. Opponents note that private corporations are exempt from public reporting requirements, and are not subject to the kinds of taxpay-er demands for information (like Freedom of Information Act requests) to which government institutions are subject.[30]

[27] Beryl Lipton, "Private prisons get taxed at a lower rate than you do," *Muckrock*, Apr. 11, 2017, https://www.muckrock.com/news/archives/2017/apr/11/private-prisons-taxes/; Ben Steverman, "How Much Americans Really Pay in Taxes," *Bloomberg*, Apr.10, 2015, https://www.bloomberg.com/news/articles/2015-04-10/how-much-americans-really-pay-in-taxes.

[28] Shapiro, *Banking on Bondage*, 18.

[29] Sasha Volokh, "Don't End Federal Private Prisons," *Washington Post*, Aug. 19, 2016, https://www.washingtonpost.com/news/volokh-conspiracy/wp/2016/08/19/dont-end-federal-private-prisons/?utm_term=.b06b3e83a709. See also Sasha Volokh, "A Tale of Two Systems: Cost, Quality, and Accountability in Private Prisons," *Harvard Law Review* 115, no. 7 (2002): 1838–68.

[30] A. Friedmann and C. Petrella, *Press Release: Organizations Urge US Rep. Sheila Jackson Lee to Reintroduce Private Prison Information Act* (Brattleboro: Human Rights Defense Center, 2012), https://www.prisonlegalnews.org/in-the-news/2012/organizations-urge -us-rep-sheila-jackson-lee-to-reintroduce-private-prison-information-act/. See also Sue Binder, *Bodies in Beds: Why Business Should Stay Out of Prisons* (New York: Algora Publishing, 2017).

One way to make sense of these debates is to see them as theoretical disputes over what constitutes a desirable or sustainable economic structure, and what kinds of social services can and should be commodified (or made into a profitable economic good) within these economic structures. Theoretical debates aside, the empirical evidence assessing these prison privatization defenses and objections is limited. For instance, in 2005, the National Institute of Justice (NIJ), a federal research agency, funded an independent cost and performance comparison between a private prison facility and three comparable, publicly operated prison facilities (all holding federal prisoners). This study, conducted by policy analysts at Abt Associates, a respected independent consulting agency, found that the private prison facility's average cost per day per prisoner was consistently as much as 15 percent lower than the public facilities average cost per day per prisoner.[31] At the same time, however, the Federal Bureau of Prisons conducted its own cost-benefit analysis and found much less impressive cost savings, of only a few percentage points.[32]

Comparing the two studies, Gerry Gaes, a visiting scientist at NIJ, noted important methodological differences that accounted for the different findings: how average populations were calculated and how much indirect operations costs, such as regional supervision and facility planning (also known as "overhead"), were allocated between the private prison facilities and the Federal Bureau of Prisons. Such careful studies reveal that cost-benefit comparisons are difficult to make rigorously, and are susceptible to methodological manipulation. These studies also reveal that the cost savings from private prisons are relatively small, at best.[33]

---

[31] Douglas C. McDonald and Kenneth Carlson, *Contracting for Imprisonment in the Federal Prison System: Cost and Performance of the Privately Operated Taft Correctional Institution* (Washington, D.C.: National Institute of Justice, Nov. 2005) (NCJ 211990), https://www.ncjrs.gov/pdffiles1/nij/grants/211990.pdf.

[32] Scott D. Camp and Dawn M. Daggett, *Evaluation of the Taft Demonstration Project: Performance of a Private-Sector Prison and the BOP* (Washington, D.C.: Federal Bureau of Prisons, Oct. 2005), https://www.bop.gov/resources/research_projects/published_reports/pub_vs_priv/orelappin2005.pdf.

[33] Gerry Gaes, "Cost, Performance Studies Look at Prison Privatization," *National Institute of Justice Journal* 259, Jun. 1, 2010, http://www.nij.gov/journals/259/pages/prison-privatization.aspx#author.

The NIJ studies are representative of other cost-benefit analyses of private prisons: scholars debate the methods underlying the studies, but the outcomes tend to reveal cost savings that are, at best, limited.[34] For insta~ in Arizona, which is one of the few states to legislatively require that priv... prisons create cost savings and to demand rigorous analyses of whether the cost savings are being achieved, evaluations found that private prisons sometimes saved a little bit over public prisons, but, in other cases, cost hundreds of dollars more per prisoner per year. Critics of the private prison companies operating in Arizona noted another problem with the cost-benefit analyses of public versus private prisons in the state: private prisons tended to accept only relatively healthy inmates, so the appearance of keeping costs down was based on the "cheap" population of prisoners these private facilities housed.[35]

Cost, however, is not the only metric by which private prisons are judged. Assault rates, healthcare provision rates, and recidivism rates all matter, too. And again, analyses comparing these rates in public and private prison facilities have produced mixed results. For instance, in the above-referenced independent study (by Abt Associates) and internal study (by the Federal Bureau of Prisons), both auditors found that the private prison facility had a lower assault rate than the public facilities, but a higher rate of drug use, escapes, and prisoner disturbances.[36]

In meta-reviews of studies of private prison facilities, the American Civil Liberties Union (2011) and the Sentencing Project (2012)— both advocacy organizations with explicitly progressive prison reform

[34] See, e.g., Brad Lundahl, Chelsea Kunz, Cyndi Brownell, Norma Harris, and Russ Van Vleet, "Prison Privatization: A Meta-analysis of Cost and Quality of Confinement Indicators," *Research on Social Work Practice* 19, no. 4 (Jul. 2009): 383–94; Dina Perrone and Travis C. Pratt, "Comparing the Quality of Confinement and Cost-Effectiveness of Public Versus Private Prisons: What We Know, Why We Do Not Know More, and Where To Go from Here," *Prison Journal* 83, no. 301 (2003): 315–16; Cody Mason, *Too Good to Be True: Private Prisons in America* (Washington, D.C.: The Sentencing Project, Jan. 2012), http://sentencingproject.org/wp-content/uploads/2016/01/Too-Good-to-be-True-Private-Prisons-in-America.pdf; Shapiro, *Banking on Bondage*.

[35] Charles L. Ryan, "Biennial Comparison of Private Versus Public Provision of Services, required per A.R.S. § 41-1609.01(K)(M)," (Phoenix: Arizona Department of Corrections, Dec. 2011), https://corrections.az.gov/sites/default/files/ars41_1609_01_biennial_comparison_report122111_e_v.pdf; Richard A. Oppel Jr., "Private Prisons Found to Offer Little in Savings," *New York Times*, May 19, 2011: A-1.

[36] See Gaes, "Cost, Performance Studies."

agendas—noted that private prison facilities across the United States had had problems with: rampant sexual abuse, appalling brutality, and inadequate provision of healthcare, all leading to documented instances of unnecessary deaths.[37] Still, private prison corporations, like CCA and GEO, argue that all prisons suffer from problems with abuse and provision of basic services, and insist (in spite of evidence to the contrary) that private prisons can save as much as 30 percent over the costs of public prison facilities.[38]

Just as with cost-benefit analyses and various measures of prison safety, comparing recidivism statistics across public and private prisons is fraught with both methodological and political challenges, and evaluations have produced inconclusive results. Even finding groups of prisoners who have been released from private prisons, for direct comparison to groups of prisoners released from public prisons can be challenging. The majority of studies evaluating private versus public prison recidivism rates have been conducted in Florida, a state that has seven privatized prison facilities and a long history of private prison contracts supported by private prison lobbyists. The first few recidivism studies conducted in Florida showed slightly lower re-arrest, re-conviction, and re-incarceration rates for prisoners from private prison facilities.[39] But a later study, which attempted to resolve many methodological challenges of earlier studies, found virtually no statistically significant differences in recidivism rates between public and private prison facilities in Florida.[40] Another study in

[37] Mason, *Too Good to Be True*, 11–12; see also Shapiro, *Banking on Bondage*.

[38] See, e.g., Matt Simmons, "Punishment & Profits: A Cost-Benefit Analysis of Private Prisons," *Oklahoma Policy Institute*, Aug. 7, 2013, http://okpolicy.org/punishment-profits-a-cost-benefit-analysis-of-private-prisons/.

[39] L. Lanza-Kaduce, K. F. Parker, and C. W. Thomas, "A Comparative Recidivism Analysis of Releasees from Private and Public Prisons," *Crime and Delinquency* 45, no. 1 (1999): 28–47; L. Lanza-Kaduce and S. Maggard, "The Long-Term Recidivism of Public and Private Prisoners," unpublished paper presented at the National Conference of the Bureau of Justice Statistics and Justice Research and Statistics Association in New Orleans, 2001; D. Farabee and Kevin Knight, *A Comparison of Public and Private Prisons in Florida: During- and Post-Prison Performance Indicators* (Los Angeles: Query Research, 2002).

[40] William Bales, Laura E. Bedard, Susan T. Quinn, David Ensley, Glen Holley, Alan Duffee, and Stephanie Sanford, *Recidivism: An Analysis of Public and Private State Prison Releases in Florida* (Tallahassee: Florida State University, Florida Department of Corrections,

Oklahoma found, by contrast, that people released from private prisons were more likely to commit new crimes, and to have higher recidivism rates than people released from public prisons.[41]

As these competing results suggest, calculating recidivism statistics presents not just a methodological challenge, but also a political one. After all, private prison companies like CCA and GEO theoretically need to establish basic metrics of success, like lower recidivism rates, in order to continue to earn government contracts. But these companies also have a contradictory incentive to keep crime rates high—just as they have incentives to keep criminal sentences long—so that their prison beds remain filled.[42] Such political motivations could, at least potentially, discourage companies from conducting recidivism studies, or encourage distortion of the analysis and presentation of study results.

Just as evaluations of private prisons—in terms of their cost savings, their ability to care for prisoners, and their recidivism outcomes—have been mixed, so have individual state experiences with specific private prison contracts. Over the course of the first twenty-five years of CCA's operation (as well as GEO's), several states, including North Carolina, Arkansas, Nevada, and California, and, most recently, the federal government, initiated and subsequently cancelled private prison contracts. Most contracts ended in frustration: private prisons did not save as much money as lawmakers had hoped, they failed to provide adequate services to prisoners, or they held prisoners too far from their home states.[43] Nonetheless, other states and, increasingly, federal agencies like Immigrations and Customs Enforcement (ICE) maintained and expanded their use of private prisons in the 2010s.

Recently, the debates about whether or not private prisons "work"— in terms of cost savings, service provision, safety, and recidivism— boiled over in a controversial U.S. federal government decision to cease

Florida Correctional Privatization Commission, Dec. 2003), NCJ 205456, http://www.dc.state.fl.us/pub/recidivismfsu/RecidivismStudy2003.PDF.

[41] Andrew L. Spivak and Susan F. Sharp, "Inmate Recidivism as a Measure of Private Prison Performance," *Criminal Justice & Behavior* 54, no. 3 (2008): 482–508.

[42] Shapiro, *Banking on Bondage*, 30.

[43] Mason, *Too Good to Be True*, 3.

contracting with private prison providers like CCA. CCA's stock price
plummeted, losing a third of its value, and critics speculated about whether the federal government's decision was a harbinger of the end of the private prison industry.[44] A closer analysis suggests that is unlikely.

BEYOND CRITIQUE: THE DEPARTMENT
OF JUSTICE RESISTS PRIVATIZATION

On August 18, 2016, Deputy Attorney General Sally Yates of the U.S.
Department of Justice (DOJ) announced that the Department would no
longer contract with private prison facilities to incarcerate federal prisoners. The short, two-page memo issued by DOJ, a federal government
agency, was clear in its assessment of private prisons: they failed to live
up to expectations. Yates wrote: "Private prisons served an important
role during a difficult period, but time has shown that they compare
poorly to our own Bureau facilities." Yates was referring to the period
in the 1990s, when, overwhelmed by population increases, the Federal Bureau of Prisons began contracting with private prisons to house
overflow prisoners. By 2013, 30,000 prisoners, making up 15 percent of
the federal prison population, were housed in private prison facilities.
While the research described in the preceding sections suggests ongoing debates about whether private prisons are cost effective, achieve rehabilitative goals, and maintain safety and security, Yates reached her
own conclusions. Private prisons, she said, have not saved the federal
government money, have not provided adequate rehabilitative program-
ming, and do not maintain adequate safety and security.[45] Yates's announcement was met with a combination of surprise, celebration, and
frustration.

[44] Geert de Lombaerde, "CCA Hammered after Word of DOJ Private-Prison Exit,"
Nashville Post, Aug. 18, 2016, http://www.nashvillepost.com/business/area-stocks/
article/20831162/cca-hammered-after-word-of-doj-privateprison-exit.

[45] Sally Q. Yates, Deputy Attorney General, "Memo for the Acting Director Federal
Bureau of Prisons: Reducing Our Use of Private Prisons," Aug. 18, 2016, https://assets.
documentcloud.org/documents/3027877/Justice-Department-memo-announcing-
announcing.pdf.

As the beginning of this chapter suggested, private prisons have been controversial since T. Don Hutto helped to open that first private immigration detention facility in Texas in 1985. But federal and state governments have continued to rely on these facilities for decades, in spite of the controversy. So what allowed Yates to make such a decisive claim about the problems with privatized prisons?

First, Yates's claim about safety and security failures was backed up by a specific report, released just a few weeks prior to her decisive memo, by the Office of the Inspector General (OIG), another federal agency within the Department of Justice. The report, *Review of the Federal Prison's Monitoring of Contract Prisons*, was damning. The executive summary noted: "[D]isturbances in several federal contract prisons resulted in extensive property damage, bodily injury, and the death of a correctional officer." Among the fourteen contract facilities evaluated, five times as many cell phones were confiscated in private facilities as in public, and rates of assault (both among prisoners and between prisoners and staff) were also significantly higher in private facilities. In at least one prison, on-site monitors found that staff had not been disciplined in *over half* of the incidents in which misconduct had been conclusively established. In two prisons, new prisoners were housed indefinitely in isolation units, for no reason other than unavailability of beds elsewhere in the facility.[46] While the general American public took little notice of this OIG report, until Yates referenced it in her surprising memo, the report followed a much better publicized exposé of a private, state prison facility.

Shane Bauer's July/August 2016 feature story in *Mother Jones*, about the four months he spent working undercover as a correctional officer at Winn Correctional Facility, a Louisiana state prison operated by CCA, provided further momentum to Yates's anti-privatization decision. In the exposé, Bauer describes the four short weeks of training he underwent to become a prison guard; on many days, he had only two hours of scheduled class, and so he just sat around and talked to the other new recruits during the remaining

---

[46] Office of the Inspector General, *Review of the Federal Prison's Monitoring of Contract Prisons* (Washington, D.C.: Department of Justice, Aug. 2016), https://oig.justice.gov/reports/2016/e1606.pdf.

eight hours. Once he got to work inside the facility, Bauer witnessed: an escape that went unnoticed by staff for hours; staff using religious beliefs as a justifications for disciplining prisoners (in violation of laws requiring the separation of church and state); day after day of cancelled programs for prisoners, in a chronically understaffed facility; unreported assaults; and serious, untreated medical conditions.[47] *Mother Jones* noted the likely role Bauer's exposé played in the Department of Justice decision to stop contracting with private prisons: "the announcement comes on the heels of a *Mother Jones* investigation that found serious deficiencies in staffing and security."[48]

Critics of private prisons, like *Mother Jones*, celebrated Yates's decision. Major national newspapers, like the *Washington Post* and *New York Times*, ran front-page stories about the decisions. Magazines like the *Atlantic* and the *New Yorker* followed up with commentaries applauding the decision. And, as noted above, CCA's stock price plummeted.

Critics quickly pointed out the limited impact of Yates's decision, however. First, it will take at least five years for the Department of Justice to conclude its multiple contracts with private prison facilities. Second, federal prisoners only account for about 13 percent of the overall U.S. prison population (210,000 out of 1.6 million), and privately held federal prisoners only account for about 17 percent of the overall population of prisoners across the United States held in private facilities (22,000 out of 131,000).[49] Third, the federal government has contracts to maintain almost the same number of immigrants in private detention centers as prisoners in private prison facilities: a total of nearly 20,000 immigrants being detained in the United States (more than 60 percent of those detained overall) are in private prison facilities.[50]

[47] Shane Bauer, "My Four Months as a Private Prison Guard," *Mother Jones*, Jul./Aug. 2016, http://www.motherjones.com/politics/2016/06/cca-private-prisons-corrections-corporation-inmates-investigation-bauer.

[48] Pema Levy, "Justice Department Plans to Stop Using Private Prisons," *Mother Jones*, Aug. 18, 2016, http://www.motherjones.com/politics/2016/08/department-justice-plans-end-private-prison.

[49] Ann Carson, *Prisoners in 2014* (Washington, D.C.: Bureau of Justice Statistics, Sept. 2015, NCJ 248955), http://www.bjs.gov/content/pub/pdf/p14.pdf.

[50] See Carson and Diaz, "Payoff" (citing Immigration and Customs Enforcement, ERO Custody Management Division. List of facilities analyzed by Grassroots Leadership from document titled "ICE Authorized Facilities Matrix," March 5, 2015).

Critics asked: if private prisons are too dangerous for prisoners, how can private detention centers, run by the same corporations, be constitutionally acceptable? The American Civil Liberties Union, for instance, explicitly noted the parallel problems with understaffing, overcrowding, and inadequate medical care that have been documented in private federal immigration detention facilities, just like those seen in private federal prison facilities.[51] Federal officials responded to the chorus of critics surprisingly quickly.

On August 29, 2016, just two weeks after Deputy Attorney General Yates announced that the federal government would end its contracts with private prison facilities, Secretary of Defense Jeh Johnson announced that the Department of Homeland Security would establish a committee to review the "current policy and practices concerning the use of private immigration detention and evaluate whether this practice should be eliminated."[52] Critics at the American Civil Liberties Union pointed out that another study was hardly necessary, and urged quicker and more decisive reform.[53] Meanwhile, investors clearly worried about the continued financial viability of the private prison industry. CCA stock prices fell even further than they had two weeks earlier, with the Federal Bureau of Prisons announcement. Over the course of August 2016, in fact, CCA shares lost half their value.

However, CCA's stock value quickly rebounded—demonstrating the company's robust size, its resilience, and, ultimately, its political influence. CCA still holds billions of dollars in both state prison contracts and federal immigration detention contracts. In fact, just days before Secretary Johnson announced that the Department of Homeland Security would re-evaluate their private prison contracts, that same agency signed

---

[51] Carl Takei, "No Review Necessary: Stop Using Private Prisons for Immigration Detention," *ACLU National Prison Project Blog*, Aug. 31, 2016, https://www.aclu.org/blog/speak-freely/no-review-necessary-stop-using-private-prisons-immigration-detention.

[52] "Statement by Secretary Jeh C. Johnson on Establishing a Review Of Privatized Immigration Detention" (Washington, D.C.: Department of Homeland Security, Aug. 29, 2016), https://www.dhs.gov/news/2016/08/29/statement-secretary-jeh-c-johnson-establishing-review-privatized-immigration.

[53] Takei, "No Review Necessary."

a $1 billion contract with CCA to build a new private detention facility.[54] Indeed, despite the foreboding signs in August 2016 (mathematically manifest in plummeting CCA stock prices), the conversation over whether and how private prisons operate remains open for debate. As one law professor and frequent *Washington Post* commentator pointed out, the evidence on private prisons remains mixed, and federal officials like Yates and Johnson seemed to have jumped to conclusions without fully implementing and completely evaluating privatization.[55]

Meanwhile, CCA leadership worked to mitigate the public damage to their name, from the OIG report and the *Mother Jones* exposé, with a major rebranding initiative: changing their name to CoreCivic, indicating an intention to diversify into a "wider range of government solutions," including prisoner re-entry programs.[56] The national nonprofit CIVIC, or Community Initiatives for Visiting Immigrants in Confinement, which seeks to end U.S. immigration detention, especially in privately run facilities, immediately filed a trademark violation action against the former CCA, for stealing the nonprofit's name, in an effort to undermine their advocacy work.[57] According to the *Wall Street Journal*, CCA's CEO explained that the name change was designed to facilitate "access to new markets in states like California that have previously resisted private-prison firms."[58] CCA's resilience suggests that many more years will pass before its business model fails, if it ever does.

Private prison companies received further political boosts later in 2016, too, with the election of Donald Trump to the American presidency.

[54] Julissa Arce, "Let's Not Take a Victory Lap on the End of Private Prisons Just Yet," *CNBC Opinion*, Aug. 22, 2016, http://www.cnbc.com/2016/08/22/lets-not-take-a-victory-lap-on-the-end-of-private-prisons-just-yet-commentary.html.

[55] Volokh, "Don't End Federal Private Prisons."

[56] See Devlin Barrett, "Private-Prison Firm CCA to Rename Itself CoreCivic," *Wall Street Journal*, Oct. 28, 2016, https://www.wsj.com/articles/private-prison-firm-cca-to-rename-itself-corecivic-1477666800; Dave Boucher, "CCA Changes Name to CoreCivic amid Ongoing Scrutiny," *The Tennessean*, Oct. 28, 2016, http://www.tennessean.com/story/news/2016/10/28/cca-changes-name-amid-ongoing-scrutiny/92883274/.

[57] CIVIC, *Press Release: Private Prison Company CCA Has Stolen the Name of a Nonprofit that Advocates Against the Use of Private Prisons*, Dec. 13, 2016, http://www.endisolation.org/blog/archives/1165.

[58] Barrett, "Private-Prison Firm CCA."

Private prison companies' stock prices "surged" with the announcement of Trump's presidential victory.[59] As of early 2017, neither the forty-fifth president nor the Department of Justice had issued any new statements about prison privatization, but the President had fired Deputy Attorney General Yates and issued executive orders designed to drastically expand federal immigration detention in the United States, an archipelago of institutions already dominated by the private prison industry.[60] Still, the negative attention to private prisons in August 2016 suggests that reform is possible, and especially that public critiques and exposés, like Shane Bauer's *Mother Jones* feature, have the power to instigate such reform.

PARTIAL PRIVATIZATION

Even if the federal government ended all of its contracts with private prison facilities, and even if each state with private prison contracts followed the federal government's lead—both unlikely events, of course—significant subsets of the prison industry would still remain privatized and, more importantly, profitable. Partial privatization raises many of the same questions about incentives and injustices that private prisons have inspired over the past few decades. While some states have resisted contracting with private prison providers, few have resisted contracting with private service providers of some kind.[61] *Partial privatization* includes a range of contracts between public prison facilities and private service providers to assist in meeting the basic needs of prisoners, including food, healthcare, and communication. Such contracts commodify both the process of incarceration and the provision of prisoners' basic needs.

---

[59] Roque Planas, "Private Prison Stocks Surge after Donald Trump Victory," *Huffington Post*, Nov. 9, 2016, http://www.huffingtonpost.com/entry/private-prison-stocks-trump_us_582336c5e4b0e80b02ce3287; Beth Reinhard, "Trump's Election Victory Gives Private Prisons a Boost," *Wall Street Journal*, Jan. 17, 2017, https://www.wsj.com/articles/trumps-election-victory-gives-private-prisons-a-boost-1484693381; James Suroweicki, "Trump Sets Private Prisons Free," *New Yorker*, Dec. 5, 2016, http://www.newyorker.com/magazine/2016/12/05/trump-sets-private-prisons-free.

[60] See Reinhard, "Trump's Election Victory."

[61] For a quick overview of profitable prison services, see Eric Markowitz, "Making Profits on the Captive Prison Market," *New Yorker*, Sept. 4, 2016, http://www.newyorker.com/business/currency/making-profits-on-the-captive-prison-market.

As in the private prison industry more generally, a few major corporations tend to dominate each of these service provision categories. For food, Aramark is the major prison provider, boasting that it serves more than one million meals a day to local jail and state prison facilities. In maximizing efficiency, Aramark minimizes costs (often to less than $2 per meal) and calories (to the bare nutritional minimum), and has been accused of serving food infested with maggots (in Ohio), or contaminated by rats (in Michigan).[62] In Michigan, correctional *officers*, not prisoners, complained not only about the low quality of the food served by Aramark, but also about the badly trained staff provided by the company.[63] Of course, for a company that provides millions of meals to prisoners each week, some shortfalls are inevitable. Nonetheless, as with fully privatized institutions, private service providers face powerful incentives to cut costs in ways that can easily become dangerous to prisoners' health and well-being.

Serious risks to physical health are even more imminent in the case of privatized healthcare providers. Corizon Correctional Healthcare (formerly Prison Health Services and Correctional Medical Services), like CCA, has existed in some form since the early 1980s. Today, Corizon contracts with more than five hundred jails and prisons across twenty-eight states to provide healthcare services.[64] Corizon's website proclaims that they serve "more prison inmates than any other private entity."[65]

[62] Christopher Zoukis and Rod L. Bower, "Aramark's Correctional Food Services: Meals, Maggots and Misconduct," *Prison Legal News*, Dec. 2, 2015, https://www.prisonlegal news.org/news/2015/dec/2/aramarks-correctional-food-services-meals-maggots-and-misconduct/. For a discussion of the low quality of prison meals, see also Alysia Santo and Lisa Iaboni, "What's in a Prison Meal?" *The Marshall Project*, July 7, 2015, https://www .themarshallproject.org/2015/07/07/what-s-in-a-prison-meal#.b1XiYRNau.

[63] SEIU Local 526M, "In-Depth: New Report Exposes Pitfalls of Prison Food Service Privatization," Mar. 31, 2016, http://www.mco-seiu.org/2016/03/31/in-depth-new-report-exposes-pitfalls-of-prison-food-service-privatization/. See the full report: Roland Zullo, *Food Service Privatization in Michigan's Prisons: Observations of Corrections Officers* (Ann Arbor: University of Michigan, Institute for Research on Labor, Employment and the Economy, 2016), http://irlee.umich.edu/wp-content/uploads/2016/06/PrivatizationOfPrisonFood.pdf.

[64] Greg Dober, "Corizon Needs a Checkup: Problems with Privatized Correctional Healthcare," *Prison Legal News*, Mar. 15, 2014, https://www.prisonlegalnews.org/news/2014/mar/15/corizon-needs-a-checkup-problems-with-privatized-correctional-healthcare/.

[65] Corizon Health, "About Corizon Health," http://www.corizonhealth.com/About-Corizon/serving-prisons.

Like CCA, Corizon has faced critiques for letting politics and ideology determine what healthcare prisoners receive, and for providing inadequate, and, in some cases, dangerously negligent care to prisoners. For instance, one Corizon nurse in Arizona was accused of contaminating multiple vials of insulin by using a dirty needle in them; Corizon officials in Florida were found guilty by a jury of systematically refusing to send prisoners to outside hospitals even when seriously ill; and Corizon healthcare providers in Idaho regularly denied food and water to chronically ill prisoners.[66]

In addition to raising ethical issues and questions about adequacy of care, the privatization of services tends to have a direct financial impact on prisoners—and their families. For instance, in many states, prisoners are required to pay in order to see a medical professional; in some states these fees are a few dollars, but Texas charges an annual flat fee of $100, plus a $3 co-pay per medical visit. At least half of the prisoners in the Texas system do not have enough money in their prisoner accounts to afford such fees, and so are forced to turn to their families, who often struggle to provide hundreds of dollars per month to support incarcerated loved ones with serious medical problems.[67]

Telephone access, which is also privatized and commodified, creates further financial hardships for prisoners and their families. Until the early 1970s, prisoners in state and federal facilities were generally permitted only one phone call every three months. Research in the 1970s first suggested that, for prisoners, maintaining some contact with their communities was a critical aspect of future rehabilitation. So, over the course of the 1970s, during the prisoners' rights movement discussed in Chapter One, prison systems gradually adopted policies of permitting prisoners to make phone calls, albeit ones that were generally monitored. Commercial payphones were installed in prisons across the United States and, at first, calling rates

[66] Beth Kutscher, "Rumble over Jailhouse Healthcare," *Modern Healthcare*, Aug. 31, 2013, http://www.modernhealthcare.com/article/20130831/MAGAZINE/308319891; Dober, "Corizon Needs a Checkup."

[67] Max Rivlin-Nadler, "How Medical Copays Haunt Prisoners and Their Loved Ones," *Vice*, Jan. 18, 2017, https://www.vice.com/en_us/article/how-medical-copays-haunt-prisoners-and-their-loved-ones.

matched those for commercial payphones outside of prison.[68] However, the prisoner communications movement basically stalled in the 1970s, even while technology moved forward. Personal phones or cell phones never became objects to which U.S. prisoners had legal access. And when new regulations granted citizens outside of prison broader rights to choose among telephone service providers, those rights were never extended to prisoners.

Today, publicly traded corporations, like Global Tel Link, contract with individual state prison systems to be the sole providers of prison phone services in a given state. This single service provider then has a monopoly on all calls from any given prison, or prison system. Moreover, all such calls from prison are "collect," charged directly to the family member to whom the call is being made. Like prisoners, prisoners' families have no choice but to use the one company providing phone service in the prison where their loved one happens to be housed.

The average cost of these calls, until recently, ranged from $10 to $30 for fifteen to twenty minutes: hundreds of times more than the cost of comparable calls between nonincarcerated people. So a family trying to keep in touch with a loved one in prison might expect to spend $100 or more per month, just to have a single, brief, weekly phone call. On average, prisoners tend to be of low socioeconomic status, to make only cents per day while working in prison, and to have families who are struggling to make ends meet, especially with one family member unable to earn an income while in prison.[69] To be more concrete: a single person living at the poverty line makes roughly $1,000 per month. At that income level, a prison phone bill of $100 consumes a full tenth of the month's income—a heavy burden indeed.

Meanwhile, private phone service providers make billions from the prison phone industry and share "kickbacks" of millions of dollars annually

[68] S. J. Jackson, "Ex-Communication: Competition and Collusion in the U.S. Prison Telephone Industry," *Critical Studies in Media Communication* 22, no.4 (2006): 263–80.

[69] See, e.g., Bruce Western and Becky Pettit, "On Mass Incarceration & Social Inequality," *Dædalus*, Summer 2010, https://www.amacad.org/content/publications/pubContent.aspx?d=808; Bruce Western, *Punishment & Inequality in America* (New York: Russell Sage Foundation, 2007).

with state governments through service contracts.[70] These gross cost inequalities, in which a subset of people are forced to pay exorbitant fees
for a service, and a corporation with a monopoly on providing that service makes significant profits, contradict basic principles of economic
justice. Indeed, an entire federal agency, the Federal Communications
Commission (FCC), exists to regulate the fair provision of communications services throughout the United States. The FCC's website
describes two of their primary goals as "promoting competition" and
"supporting the nation's economy by ensuring an appropriate competi-
tive framework for the unfolding of the communications revolution."[71]
So how did prison phone service providers establish this kind of monopoly, and how has it persisted?

It all began in 1984—right around the time private prisons were born.
Private prisons met a growing need for more prisoner beds as incarceration rates increased across the United States, and private phone companies met a growing need for more phone calls between those prisoners
and their families. However, the direct impetus for the monopolistic
contracts that created such high calling costs is a bit counterintuitive: the
contracts actually followed on the heels of the *disintegration* of AT&T's
monopoly over the entire U.S. telephone industry. As new telephone companies scrambled to establish niche markets, many signed contracts with
individual state prison and county jail systems. At first the competition
was steep, but over time the incentives turned out to be all wrong. Steven
Jackson has eloquently described the perverse incentives:

> [C]ounty, state, and federal officials have entered into what
> amount to profit-sharing agreements with telephone service
> providers . . . Under such conditions, the incentives of price

---

[70] Drew Kukorowski, *The Price to Call Home: State Sanctioned Monopolization of the
Prison Phone Industry* (Northhampton: Prison Policy Initiative, 2012), https://www
.prisonpolicy.org/phones/report.html; see also Prison Phone Justice, "Fighting for the
Right to Call Home," video available online at: http://nationinside.org/campaign/
prison-phone-justice/.

[71] Federal Communications Commission, "What We Do," https://www.fcc.gov/about-fcc/
what-we-do.

> competition have worked in precisely the opposite direction,
> with companies offering the highest bids (in terms of rates
> and commissions) routinely awarded contracts, the costs of
> which are passed on to the (literally) captive market.[72]

In other words, as long as prison systems are choosing who will provide phone services to prisoners, they have every incentive for those phone services to be as expensive as possible, so that the prison system can share the ample profits with the prison phone companies. And, of course, since prisoners have no choice about how, when, and where they make their phone calls, there is no viable competition to drive down high calling costs. Some have argued that this monopoly has incentivized a black market in cell phones smuggled into prison. The high prevalence of contraband cell phones in prison suggests that such a black market indeed exists (and likely further exacerbates the risks and costs associated with prisoners trying to call home).[73]

Within ten years of the disintegration of the AT&T monopoly, prisoners' families were organizing to fight for better regulation of prison phone costs, but the industry is so profitable that prison providers have been persistent in their efforts to resist any regulation. In February of 2000, prisoner family members filed a class action lawsuit (in a federal district court in Washington, D.C.) alleging that high prison phone calling rates actually violated their constitutional rights: to free speech and association, to equal protection under the law, and to freedom of contract.[74] The lead plaintiff was Martha Wright-Reed, then a nurse in her seventies, who had sought to keep in touch with her grandson over a decade of his incarceration. In that time, she had seen the monthly cost of a few ten-to-fifteen-minute phone calls increase from

---

[72] Jackson, "Ex-Communication," 269.

[73] Campaign for Prison Phone Justice, "FCC Field Hearing Attempts to Focus Prison Phone Conversation on Contraband Cellphones," Apr. 5, 2016, https://nationinside. org/campaign/prison-phone-justice/posts/fcc-field-hearing-attempts-to-focus-prison-phone-conversation-on-contraband-cellphones/.

[74] Center for Constitutional Rights, "Historic Case: *Martha Wright v. Corrections Corporation of America* (FCC Petition)," https://ccrjustice.org/home/what-we-do/our-cases/martha-wright-v-corrections-corporation-america-fcc-petition.

$50 per month to over $200 per month. She had spent thousands of dollars trying to maintain a single familial connection. Her grandson said sometimes he would call just "so she could hear my voice," even though he knew his grandmother "couldn't afford to pick up" that week, or month. The 2000 lawsuit was full of such stories of families unable to afford the cost of even saying "hello" or "I love you" to a sister, father, daughter, or grandson in prison.[75] The judge who reviewed the class action complaint immediately referred it to the Federal Communications Commission, reasoning that the FCC was in the best position to write new regulations to resolve the prison phone rate problem across the United States.[76]

For years, though, the FCC ignored the families petitioning for relief from the insurmountable costs of keeping in touch with their incarcerated relatives. In 2012, the *Washington Post* noted that 3,500 days had passed without a response from the FCC; the family members' petition was about to "celebrate its tenth anniversary." Finally, in 2013, the FCC began to consider serious reform to prison calling rates.

In August of 2013, the regulatory agency passed caps on interstate, or long distance, calling rates: 0.12 to 0.25 cents per minute for various kinds of calls. The caps reduced the average $17 cost of a fifteen-minute call from prison to no more than $2 or $3. And the FCC clearly stated that charges should actually be based on the costs of services provided, rather than on commissions and contract bonuses negotiated between prison systems and phone providers.[77] This regulation constrained prison phone service provider charges, and promised instant relief to family members like Martha Wright-Reed, whose grandson was in federal prison in a different state. But the regulation was also functionally limited in its application— to long distance calls made across state lines. The vast majority of U.S.

[75] Justin Moyer, "After Almost a Decade, FCC Has Yet to Rule On High Cost of Prison Phone Calls," *Washington Post*, Dec. 2, 2012, https://www.washingtonpost.com/opinions/after-almost-a-decade-fcc-has-yet-to-rule-on-high-cost-of-prison-phone-calls/2012/12/02/b11ea164-2daf-11e2-9ac2-1c61452669c3_print.html.

[76] Center for Constitutional Rights, "Historic Case."

[77] Marc Wigfield, "Press Release: FCC Bars High Rates for Long Distance Phone Calls in Jails and Prisons Nationwide" (Washington, D.C.: Federal Communications Commission, Aug. 9, 2013), https://apps.fcc.gov/edocs_public/attachmatch/DOC-322749A1.pdf.

prisoners, however, are housed in state prison systems, and remain subject to high calling rates for *within* state, or local, communications.

In 2015, the FCC attempted to address the high costs of more local calls, too, issuing caps on the per-minute costs of *all* calls from prisons and jails. But the prison phone service industry resisted, filing a lawsuit in which they argued that the new rates violated existing contracts, and did not account for the high costs of providing phone services in a variety of different secure facilities, especially smaller facilities.[78] Initially, a federal judge issued a *stay*—an order to delay implementation of the caps on prison phone calling rates until a court could more carefully consider the legal arguments made by prison phone service providers.

In response, the FCC, which was finally engaged in the question of high prison calling rates, reassert the importance of lowering rates. In an August 2016 press release, the FCC announced revised rate caps, allowing prison phone service providers in smaller institutions to charge slightly higher rates for services, but reasserting the importance of the overall reforms. From the title to the justification, the press release announcing the new rates read more like a legal brief in defense of the FCC's actions than a description of a new regulation: "FCC Adopts Affordable, Sustainable Inmate Calling Rates" in order to implement "just, reasonable, and fair" rates on behalf of "society's most vulnerable . . . people trying to stay in touch with loved ones serving time in jail or prison."[79] The new caps were scheduled to go into effect in 2017.

As with the value of CCA's stock, the election of Donald Trump again changed the landscape of prison privatization and profitmaking. In this case, the president appointed a new, Republican chairman of the FCC. Days later, the FCC notified the federal, D.C. Circuit court considering the intrastate regulations that the Commission no longer intended to defend either the intrastate rate cap or the reasoning behind the proposed rates. Nonetheless, because so many other advocacy organizations were

[78] John Brodkin, "In Blow to Inmates' Families, Court Halts New Prison Phone Rate Caps," *Ars Technica*, Mar. 7, 2016, arstechnica.com/tech-policy/2016/03/in-blow-to-inmates-families-court-halts-new-prison-phone-rate-caps/.

[79] Federal Communications Commission, "Inmate Telephone Service," Aug. 10, 2016, https://www.fcc.gov/consumers/guides/inmate-telephone-service.

already involved in the litigation, the court has indicated that it will still consider the legality of the rate caps. As of 2017, the regulations capping prison-calling rates within states remained in legal limbo.[80]

Likewise, prisoners remain a captive and vulnerable market. And corporations, which have developed lucrative businesses capitalizing on the prisoner market, remain invested in finding alternative means of profiting from prisons. As with the privatization of both prisons and various services within prisons, prison phone service providers have proven both persistent and creative. Most recently, they have been working with local prison and jail facilities to cultivate exclusive contracts for video visitation services.

At first, video visitation sounds like a great idea. Video calls would allow prisoners to not only talk to their loved ones, but to see them face to face, even if the family member could not travel in person to visit the prisoner. And video calling would update the old-fashioned pay phone technology in prisons, bringing the communications infrastructure into the twenty-first century.

Of course the reality is not so simple. The exclusive contracts for video visitation, especially in jails, often require a given facility to replace in-person visitation with video visitation, actually reducing the quality and availability of prisoners' communications with their families.[81] And video visitation is not subject to the cost caps that the FCC has implemented on phone calls, so prisoners and their families are again vulnerable to the "excessive rates and egregious fees" the FCC has been attempting to reign in.[82]

---

[80] Zoe Tillman, "The FCC Has Stopped Defending Its Own Rules Lowering the Cost of Prisoner Phone Calls," *Buzzfeed*, Feb. 6, 2017, https://www.buzzfeed.com/zoetillman/the-fcc-has-stopped-defending-its-own-rules-lowering-the-cos?utm_term=.edv34QzXv#.yxl83V0DB.

[81] See, e.g., Hamed Aleaziz, "Want to Visit an Inmate? Increasingly, You'll Have to Log On," *San Francisco Chronicle*, Feb. 24, 2015, www.sfgate.com/crime/article/Want-to-visit-an-inmate-increasingly-you-ll-6095576.php.

[82] Bernadette Rabuy and Peter Wagner, *Screening Out Family Time: The For-Profit Video Visitation in Industry in Prisons and Jails* (Northampton: Prison Policy Initiative, Jan. 2015), www.prisonpolicy.org/visitation/report.html; FCC, "Inmate Telephone Service."

In sum, prisons are expensive institutions to operate, and prisoners have a seemingly endless range of rights and needs—from the need for a bed to sleep in, food to eat, and basic healthcare, to the need to communicate with family members. Providing this range of services to a growing population of prisoners presents challenges to local, state, and federal governments.

Private corporations have argued that they can ease these challenges and provide cost-efficient services. Critics argue that private corporations have failed to provide effective services, have prioritized profits over justice, or, worse, have sought to intervene and redefine constitutional rights to create profitable punishments, whether in the form of more detention, longer sentences, or more expensive communication. Reformers are left to insist on the maintenance of existing basic rights, to resist increases in punishments, and to justify decreasing profits.

A state-run institution, like a prison, has obligations to fulfill public goals of protecting public safety and legal goals of meeting the basic needs of the institutionalized. In contrast, a privately run corporation, like CCA or Global Tel Link, has obligations to partners, stockholders, and employees to run an efficient business and to maximize profits. When private corporations take over state institutions, the public and legal obligations of running a government agency sometimes conflict with the financial obligations of running a business. In too many cases, these conflicts are inadequately regulated, as with the high fees the phone service industry charges to prisoners and their families, or the private prison industry's understaffing of its institutions. Both examples represent reasonable economic choices, which nonetheless jeopardize governmental goals of meeting prisoners' basic needs and maintaining institutional safety. As both the private prison industry and the prison phone service monopolies discussed in this chapter have revealed, mixing up profits and justice raises tough questions about basic human rights, ethics, economics.

CONCLUSION

In the 2010s, preliminary statistics suggest that mass incarceration might be on the decline. Many of the states with the biggest increases in their rates of incarceration (and in sheer numbers of people incarcerated) over the 1980s and 1990s have cut back their prison populations significantly. For instance, California has reduced its prison population from a peak of 163,000 prisoners in 2006 (which prompted the U.S. Supreme Court to find the state's prisons were so unconstitutionally overcrowded that one prisoner a week was dying unnecessarily) to a population under 128,000 prisoners in 2016.[1] And Texas has reduced its prison population from a peak of 173,000 prisoners in 2010 to a population under 143,000 prisoners in 2016.[2] These states mirror national trends; the overall U.S. prison population peaked in 2009 and 2010 and has either remained stable or fallen in subsequent years.[3]

Critiques of both mass incarceration and the associated harsh conditions of confinement are increasingly widespread and politically bipartisan. A growing social and political consensus frames these punishment policies as both expensive and ineffective. One of the early products of this consensus was the Prison Rape Elimination Act, passed in 2003, with strong bipartisan support, to study, analyze, and reduce the problem of rape in prison. Another consensus law was the Second Chance

---

[1] For an archive of California prison population reports, see "Weekly Total Population Report Archive," California Department of Corrections and Rehabilitation, http://www.cdcr.ca.gov/Reports_Research/Offender_Information_Services_Branch/Weekly Wed/Weekly_Wednesday_Tpop1a_Archive.html. The overcrowding case was *Brown v. Plata*, 563 U.S. 493 (2011).

[2] Jolie McCullough, "Dip in Texas Prison Population Continues Trend," *Texas Tribune*, Sept. 25, 2015, https://www.texastribune.org/2015/09/25/slight-dip-in-texas-prisoner-population-trend/.

[3] E. Ann Carson, *Prisoners in 2014* (Washington, D.C.: Bureau of Justice Statistics, 2015), http://www.bjs.gov/content/pub/pdf/p14.pdf.

Act, passed in 2007, again with strong bipartisan support, to invest in helping the formerly incarcerated reintegrate into their communities.[4] In both cases, the laws mixed arguments about religious values with arguments about constitutional rights and cost-effective social investment, suggesting that prison (and mass incarceration) reform could be popular among surprisingly varied interest groups. For instance, goals of eliminating prison rape and investing in second chances appeal to religious groups, who object to same-sex intercourse and believe in redemption; to civil rights groups, who believe in maintaining control over one's body and maximizing the availability of citizenship rights; and to fiscal conservatives, who believe in preventing social violence and reducing recidivism.

The Obama administration's "smart on crime" initiative built on this bipartisan consensus. The initiative focused on efficient and fair crime control, discouraging federal prosecutors from automatically charging defendants with the most serious offense, encouraging individualized assessments of defendants to focus attention and resources on the most serious cases, and avoiding wasting prosecutorial and punitive resources on less serious cases.[5] Not only did the administration seek prospective reforms, but they worked to apply these reforms retroactively—soliciting and reviewing clemency petitions from prisoners with demonstrated good behavior, who would not have ever received such long sentences under the administration's new smart-on-crime policies. In all, between 2014 and 2017, then-president Obama granted 1,715 petitions for clemency (including to 568 prisoners with life sentences), more than the last twelve presidents combined.[6] And Obama weighed in on prison conditions, too,

[4] See National PREA Resource Center, "Prison Rape Elimination Act," https://www.prearesourcecenter.org/about/prison-rape-elimination-act-prea; Office of Justice Programs, "Second Chance Act (SCA)," https://www.bja.gov/ProgramDetails.aspx?Program_ID=90.

[5] See Barack Obama, "Commentary: The President's Role in Advancing Criminal Justice Reform," *Harvard Law Review* 130, no. 3 (Jan. 2017): 811–66; United States Department of Justice, "Attorney General's Smart on Crime Initiative," https://www.justice.gov/ag/attorney-generals-smart-crime-initiative.

[6] Gregory Korte, "Obama grants 330 more commutations, bringing total to a record 1,715," *USA Today*, Jan. 19, 2017; United States Department of Justice, "Clemency Statistics," https://www.justice.gov/pardon/clemency-statistics.

becoming the first sitting president to visit a federal prison. He also issued regulations to ban solitary confinement for juveniles, and to limit its use in other federal contexts.[7]

However, Obama's reforms were limited. More than 10,000 clemency petitions from nonviolent drug offenders were denied or closed without presidential action, and tens of thousands of prisoners continue to serve decades-long criminal sentences (many for drug crimes) in federal prison. That does not even count the hundreds of thousands of comparably situated state prisoners. Likewise, only a few juveniles were ever subject to solitary confinement in the federal prison system, but thousands remain in solitary confinement in state prisons. However limited, Obama's federal reforms have both symbolic and precedential value.

Scholars have interpreted this network of decarceration trends differently. For instance, political scientist Marie Gottschalk, in *Caught: The Prison State and the Lockdown of American Politics*, argues that mass incarceration has always been about political oppression, and reform will require new investments in different political systems and moral values.[8] Legal scholar Hadar Aviram, on the other hand, has argued that economic crises have driven reform, and divesting from mass incarceration is, indeed, an important step forward.[9] Criminologists Todd Clear and Natasha Frost explain the turn away from mass incarceration in terms of a dawning social awareness that tough-on-crime policies, rather than increasingly severe criminal acts or spiking crime rates, caused mass incarceration.[10] As this book has sought to show, all of these factors—politics, law and economics, increasing social awareness, and

---

[7] Barack Obama, "Why We Must Rethink Solitary Confinement," *Washington Post*, Jan. 25, 2016, https://www.washingtonpost.com/opinions/barack-obama-why-we-must-rethink-solitary-confinement/2016/01/25/29a361f2-c384-11e5-8965-0607e0e265ce_story.html?utm_term=.2822bdfafb84.

[8] Marie Gottshcalk, *Caught: The Prison State and the Lockdown of American Politics* (Princeton: Princeton University Press, 2015).

[9] Hadar Aviram, *Cheap on Crime: Recession Era Politics and the Transformation of American Punishment* (Berkeley: University of California Press, 2015).

[10] Todd R. Clear and Natasha A. Frost, *The Punishment Imperative: The Rise and Failure of Mass Incarceration in America* (New York: New York University Press, 2013).

others—are important to making sense of punishment policy and mass incarceration practices.

As of 2017, however, a new president has brought new perspectives to the topic of mass incarceration and the prospects for decarceration. If Todd Clear and Natasha Frost thought Americans in 2013 had revealed a new understanding of the difference between criminal activity (which steadily decreased in the late twentieth century) and criminalization policy (which steadily increased in the late twentieth century), politics in 2017, just four years later, suggest otherwise. In January of 2017, President Donald Trump issued an executive order banning immigrants from seven primarily Muslim countries from the United States—claiming the order was necessary for national security, because immigrants cause crime and terrorism. And Congress confirmed a new attorney general: Senator Jeff Sessions, who proclaimed a "crime problem" of permanently rising crime rates.[11] A robust body of social science research rebuts both claims: on average, immigrants commit fewer crimes than native-born citizens, and U.S. crime rates are stable or declining.[12] Nevertheless, such public claims by national leaders raise the specter of a *phantom crime wave*, which might justify a return to longer prison sentences and harsher prison policies, or a retrenchment of mass incarceration.

One way this might happen is through a new kind of transinstitutionalization, echoing the shift of institutionalized people, between the 1950s and the 1990s, from locked psychiatric care facilities

---

[11] See, e.g., Adolfo Flores, "Without Evidence, Trump Blames Chicago Violence on Undocumented Immigrants," *BuzzFeed News*, Feb. 8, 2017, https://www.buzzfeed.com/adolfoflores/without-evidence-trump-blames-chicago-violence-on-undocument?utm_term=.xmjeJOvod#.cpoX8LOQj; Alex Shephard, "Donald Trump and Jeff Sessions Are Going to Use an Imaginary Crime Wave to Launch a Crackdown," *New Republic*, Jan. 9, 2017, https://newrepublic.com/minutes/140549/donald-trump-jeff-sessions-going-use-imaginary-crime-wave-launch-crackdown.

[12] See Charis Kubrin, Graham C. Ousey, Lesley Reid, and Robert Adelman, "Immigrants Do Not Increase Crime, Research Shows," *Scientific American*, Feb. 7, 2017, https://www.scientificamerican.com/article/immigrants-do-not-increase-crime-research-shows/; Lori Robertson, "Dueling Claims on Crime Trend," *Factcheck.org*, Jul. 3, 2016, http://www.factcheck.org/2016/07/dueling-claims-on-crime-trend/.

into locked punitive facilities, as described in Chapter Two. Now, in the 2010s, individual state systems and bipartisan federal initiatives—from the *Plata* litigation discussed in Chapter One to the "smart on crime" initiatives discussed above—have facilitated reductions in the populations of prisons and jails. But simultaneous initiatives facilitated increases in the populations of other locked facilities, especially immigrant detention centers. Indeed, President Trump has pledged vast expansions in both the number of immigrants detained and deported and in the institutional space to house these detainees. As Chapter Five described, many corporations, from private prison companies like CCA and GEO Group to prison service providers like Aramark and Global Tel Link, would certainly welcome increased investments in detention space. So even if reductions in federal and state prison populations continued, the absolute number of people detained in some kind of locked facility might remain relatively stable—or even increase.

Still, local level reform and decarceration initiatives persist. For instance, throughout the fall of 2016, prisoners in state systems across the United States engaged in work stoppages to protest prison labor, prison conditions, and mass incarceration.[13] In January of 2017, prisoners in Delaware organized an uprising to protest conditions, taking over a prison and holding staff hostage. One officer died.[14] At the same time some Americans voted for Trump (expressing support for his anti-crime, anti-poor, anti-immigrant agenda), others voted to legalize marijuana (in California, Massachusetts and Nevada), to reduce prison sentences for certain crimes (in California and Oklahoma), and to reform bail procedures to protect those people too poor to afford to post money to secure

---

[13] Amy Goodman and Denis Moynihan, "Solidarity from Solitary: The National Prison Strike," *Democracy Now*, Sept. 29, 2017, https://www.democracynow.org/2016/9/29/solidarity_from_solitary_the_national_prison; E. Tammy Kim, "A National Strike Against Prison Slavery," *New Yorker*, Oct. 3, 2016.

[14] Mark Berman and Katie Mettier, "Hostage Standoff in Delaware Prison Ends with One Corrections Officer Dead," *Washington Post*, Feb. 2, 2017, https://www.washingtonpost.com/news/morning-mix/wp/2017/02/02/inmates-demanding-education-protesting-trump-take-hostages-at-delaware-prison/?utm_term=.5c543afb1f81.

their release from jail pending trial (in New Mexico).[15] In many other states, legislators and administrators are considering similar policies. In fact, scholars across the social sciences have argued for the importance of thinking about criminal justice innovation and reform at the local level— where the majority of criminal justice policy-making power exists, where the majority of criminal justice funding is controlled, and where the majority of people convicted of crimes are punished.[16] With local-level reform, citizens confront policies that directly affect them, in their back-yards and neighborhoods.

This book has sought to demonstrate how the increasing *visibility* (and relevance) of mass incarceration and its many detrimental consequences has contributed to both the search for alternatives and the divestment from at least some abusive policies (like the exorbitant fines and fees levied on citizens in Ferguson, Missouri, as described in Chapter Three). Indeed, each of the five chapters at the core of the book has examined the relationship between rights and visibility. When Larry Hope asserted his right to be free from cruel and unusual punishment, the harms he had suffered made national news. When the doctor assigned to review Joseph Duran's death revealed how Duran had suffered and prison offi-cials had sought to hide that suffering, judges paid close attention. When Howard Dean Bailey got deported for a minor and old drug conviction, his family suffered the consequences, and their suffering amplified the problems many parents, siblings, and children have suffered as a result of

[15] German Lopez, "The Case for Optimism on Criminal Justice Reform—Even under President Trump," *Vox*, Nov. 10, 2016, http://www.vox.com/policy-and-politics/2016/11/10/13580644/president-trump-criminal-justice-2016.

[16] See, e.g., Vanessa Barker, *The Politics of Imprisonment: How the Democratic Process Shapes the Way America Punishes Offenders* (New York: Oxford University Press, 2009); Michael Campbell, "Politics, Prisons, and Law Enforcement: An Examination of the Emergence of 'Law and Order' Politics in Texas," *Law and Society Review* 45 (2011): 631–61; Ruth Wilson Gilmore, *Golden Gulag: Prisons, Surplus, Crisis, and Opposition in Globalizing California* (Berkeley: University of California Press, 2007); Mona Lynch, *Sunbelt Justice: Arizona and the Transformation of American Punishment* (Stanford: Stanford University Press, 2009); Judah Schept, "'A Lockdown Facility . . . with the Feel of a Small, Private College': Liberal Politics, Jail Expansion, and the Carceral Habitus," *Theoretical Criminology* 17 (2013): 71–88.

a loved one's criminal conviction. When people like Eileen Janis are disenfranchised in large numbers, the potential effect on election outcomes
attracts the attention of politicians and political parties. And when prisoners go to private jail facilities, or incur the costs of privatized services,
stock prices become visibly intertwined with incarceration rates and service provision policies.

Social science analyses of rights limitations have further contributed
to the visibility of the prison system. Sociologists and psychologists alike
have documented the lived experience of incarceration—including the
health risks of harsh or abusive conditions of incarceration. Historians
and political scientists have revealed the racially disparate impact of
social policies marginalizing and stigmatizing the formerly incarcerated,
and questioned how votes are distributed within communities. Economists have evaluated the costs and benefits of privatizing institutions and
institutional service delivery. In sum, the studies discussed throughout
this book, together, contribute to efforts to make mass incarceration more
visible, more transparent, and, therefore, more susceptible to reform. To
the extent that mass incarceration has been rendered visible through the
mounting evidence, explored in this book, of the ways in which prisoners
have been isolated and abused, silenced and extorted, mass incarceration
will be harder to obfuscate, forget, or erase, even as new policies of detention propose changes to its form.

Throughout many of the narratives presented in these pages, rights
limitations, like the Prison Litigation Reform Act or automatic deportation or disenfranchisement, not only hinder the visibility of mass incarceration but also facilitate institutional opacity. For instance, institutions
like Joseph Duran's "mental health crisis bed" are not only hidden from
the public eye, but blacked out, resistant to media or judicial oversight. In
fact, the many hidden aspects of mass incarceration explored in this book
share a common cause: lack of transparency.

This common cause, in turn, suggests that transparency should be a
critical principle of any new alternative to mass incarceration. Transparency in governance is foundational to democracy: in order for citizens
to share in governance decisions, they must know who is making what

decisions and why. And, of course, citizens of democracies share in the costs of government through paying taxes—which fund governmental institutions from prisons to hospitals to deportation regimes.

In order to control the tendencies towards abuse and exploitation revealed throughout this volume, data must be collected; prisons must be open to visitors and politicians and journalists; and policies must be regularly and publicly evaluated. Instead of taking social scientists and policymakers by surprise, as the onset of mass incarceration did, perhaps the next major turn in punishment policy will better incorporate social science and policy insights.

TIMELINE OF KEY LAWS, CASES, AND EVENTS

- 1791: Bill of Rights (including Eighth Amendment) ratified
- 1871: *Ruffin v. Commonwealth*, a Virginia Supreme Court case, notes that, according to the Thirteenth Amendment, prisoners are slaves of the state
- 1890 [through 1960s]: Jim Crow laws enacted in the American South
- 1953: Federal habeas corpus rights expanded to include both challenges to the place of confinement (in a case in the Washington, D.C. Circuit Court, *Miller v. Overholser*) and challenges to state habeas corpus decisions (in a U.S. Supreme Court case, *Brown v. Allen*)
- 1962: *Robinson v. California* decided; U.S. Supreme Court establishes that Eighth Amendment rights apply to state, criminal codes.
- 1963: President Kennedy signs the Community Mental Health Act into law, designed to replace locked psychiatric facilities with community mental health centers
- 1964: *Cooper v. Pate* decided; U.S. Supreme Court establishes that prisoners may bring Section 1983 civil rights claims to challenge their treatment in prison
- 1965: Voting Rights Act passed; nearly universalizes suffrage

- 1972: Geraldo Rivera's exposé of the Willowbrook State School on Staten Island airs on national television
- 1973: Consent decree in *Hook v. Arizona* (in federal district court) protects state prisoners' First Amendment rights to receive mail
- 1975: *O'Connor v. Donaldson* decided; U.S. Supreme Court establishes the "danger to self or others" standard for civil confinement of the mentally ill
- 1978: *Hutto v. Finney* decided; U.S. Supreme court upholds application of Eighth Amendment to Arkansas prison conditions
- 1983: Corrections Corporation of America (CCA) founded; T. Don Hutto is a director
- 1984–5:
  - CCA establishes first private jail facility (in Tennessee) and first private detention facility (in Texas)
  - U.S. Supreme Court establishes qualified immunity for prison officials in *Cleavinger v. Saxner*
- 1986: CCA becomes a publicly traded corporation
- 1995: Larry Hope is tied to a hitching post in Alabama
- 1994: U.S. Supreme Court establishes the legal standard of "deliberate indifference," which effectively protects prison officials from litigation, in *Farmer v. Brennan*
- 1996: The Prison Litigation Reform Act passes
- 1997: The Adoption and Safe Families Act passes
- 2000: Family members of prisoners file a federal lawsuit (*Wright v. Corrections Corporation of America*, in a Washington, D.C. court) to seek caps on prison phone calling rates
- 2002:
  - *Hope v. Pelzer* decided; U.S. Supreme Court finds no qualified immunity available for the prison officials who tied Larry Hope to a hitching post
  - *Sauvé v. Canada* (decided by the Canadian Supreme Court) invalidates blanket prisoner disenfranchisement legislation in Canada, setting an international precedent

- 2004: Eric Cadora maps "million dollar blocks"
- 2005: *Hirst v. the United Kingdom* decided; the European Court of Human Rights invalidates blanket restrictions on prisoner voting in the United Kingdom
- 2008:
  - Eileen Janis turned away from voting in South Dakota.
  - Benjamin Fleury-Steiner publishes *Dying Inside*, which describes egregious mistreatment of HIV-positive prisoners in Limestone Correctional Facility in Alabama, where Larry Hope had been tied to a hitching post.
  - Financial crisis, attributed to lack of financial regulation, especially in the mortgage industry, peaks
- 2010:
  - Maria Rivera receives a bill from Orange County for $16,372, the cost of her juvenile son's incarceration
  - *Frodl v. Austria* decided; the European Court of Human Rights invalidates blanket restrictions on prisoner voting in Austria
- 2011: *Plata v. Brown* is decided; the U.S. Supreme Court upholds a population reduction order for California prisons
- 2012: Howard Dean Bailey deported to Jamaica
- 2013:
  - 30,000 prisoners in California refuse food for as long as sixty days to protest conditions in solitary confinement
  - Joseph Duran dies in a "mental health crisis bed" at California's Mule Creek State Prison
  - The American Bar Association initiates the National Inventory of the Collateral Consequences of Conviction
  - Federal Communications Commission (FCC) passes caps on prison phone calling rates across state lines
- 2014: Police officer Darren Wilson (white) shoots unarmed, 18-year-old Michael Brown (black) in Ferguson, Missouri
- 2015:
  - *Ashker v. Brown* case settles in a federal district court in California; indefinite solitary confinement banned in the state

- ○ Department of Justice (DOJ) releases report documenting systematic civil rights violations in Ferguson, Missouri Police Department
- ○ FCC attempts to regulate intrastate (within state) prison phone calling rates
- 2016:
  - ○ *Rivera v. Orange County* decided; the Ninth Circuit Court of Appeals discharges Maria Rivera's debt for her juvenile son's incarceration in Orange County, California
  - ○ DOJ announces settlements in 2005–07 securities fraud cases
  - ○ DOJ announces it is ending federal contracts with private prison corporations

INDEX